The Culture Factory

Walter Santagata

The Culture Factory

Creativity and the Production of Culture

Springer

Prof. Walter Santagata
University of Turin
Dipartimento di Economia "Cognetti de Martiis"
Via Po 53
10123 Torino
Italy
walter.santagata@unito.it

Translator
Susan Finnel
Via des Ambrois 2
10123 Torino
Italy
su_dav@libero.it

1) Originally published under the title "La fabbrica della cultura" by Società editrice il Mulino, Bologna, Italy, 2007
2) Translation into English: Susan Finnel

ISBN 978-3-642-13357-2 e-ISBN 978-3-642-13358-9
DOI 10.1007/978-3-642-13358-9
Springer Heidelberg Dordrecht London New York

Library of Congress Control Number: 2010934757

Cover design: WMXDesign GmbH, Heidelberg, Germany

Printed on acid-free paper

Springer is part of Springer Science+Business Media (www.springer.com)

Silvia, per la vita
1974–2006

ὃν οἱ θεοὶ φιλοῦσιν ἀποθνήσκει νέος
Menander

Acknowledgment

Some of the chapters in this book appear in print for the first time while others are reworkings of previously published essays written in recent years. I am grateful to my co-authors for their generous willingness to review texts on which we collaborated and to the friends and colleagues with whom I discussed many of the issues I deal with. My gratitude to Susan Finnel, who has been not only a translator, but also a careful reader and considerate counselor.

Preface

Since the publication of the Italian edition, this has been a fortunate book. It is not easy to move ideas from the desk of an economist or sociologist to the desk of the Minister of Culture and this usually involves protracted mediation by think tanks, experts and political advisers. Actually the idea of working on a white paper on creativity, suggested in the *Conclusions*, first saw the light as the goal of a national commission of the Italian Ministry of Culture and afterwards became the subject of a book (Santagata 2009). It was after my experience working on the committee and writing the book that I decided to add a new chapter to this English edition: *Two models of creativity: technological innovation and social quality*. In it I develop the idea that creativity is vital not only because as a stimulus to technological innovation, but also, and in some countries even more importantly, because of its contribution to *social quality*.

A distinguishing characteristic of this new edition is the greater attention paid to the implementation of policies that encourage the production of creativity-based goods and services. Developing countries' vast reservoir of idle creativity and traditional culture could enable them to nurture a new model of local economic and social growth which deserves to be rediscovered and re-launched.

A further concern is the worldwide growth of the Internet. This development has modified the traditional linearity of the value chain of production of cultural goods, namely the ways artists are selected and works of art are conceived, produced, conserved, distributed and consumed. What is emerging is a new figure, the *prosumer*, a neologism indicating the blurring that has occurred between the roles of producer and consumer of artworks. *User generated contents* and *virtuality* are modifying the business models of culture and the old distinction between consumption and production.

I hope this English edition will reach new readers and inspire scholars and students in cultural economics. This will be a tangible sign of the usefulness of my work.

La Mortola, Italy W. Santagata
May 2010

Contents

Chapter 1
Introduction: Questions that Came from Afar

Torino, Italy, 2007

Long silences – too long, like pauses waiting to be filled – showed that a host of questions was spinning through his mind. He had waited to ask them, because he wanted to be sure he did not seem incautious. He was dressed a bit oddly but the long cloak and slouch hat he wore, international street-à-porter, aroused neither attention nor curiosity.

He had witnessed a crescendo of wonders. The man of genius was astonished and it showed on his intense, austere visage. Technology had always fascinated him. His imagination had been the liveliest, the most penetrating of his times but the applications he was now seeing went far beyond anything he could have imagined. Self-propelled machines, devices that spoke, living statues – it was all incredible. But watching people standing on line waiting to enter the Galleria Sabauda art museum the questions resurfaced and he still could not find answers.

The most touching moment had been when in the dimly lit underground chamber of the Royal Library he had seen his self-portrait again. He couldn't touch it because of the thick protective glass. He wondered why it was there, but suddenly the memory of that long-ago day filled his mind. He recalled the sheet of white paper that came to life as he drew, a line, another line – living image of living matter. The mouth, the nose. And then, as though looking into double mirrors that endlessly multiply images, there were the eyes staring into his, scrutinizing the mind's infinite depth. The long white hair and flowing beard made the face undulate in the semidarkness, a Zen island in a sea with waves of sand, going beyond the edges of the paper, transcending its physical limits. Through the sheet of paper, the miracle of the air that caressed that face, that reanimated the features of a strong, questioning spirit was recreated.

The Royal Library had some Michelangelo drawings and seeing them was a great pleasure, but then he was too overcome by emotion to continue. They took him to historic Caffè Fiorio for a moment's pause and some rest. His journey from the past had consumed all his energies, but the delicious beverage he sipped was

W. Santagata, *The Culture Factory*,
DOI 10.1007/978-3-642-13358-9_1, © Springer-Verlag Berlin Heidelberg 2010

prodigious. The coffee helped him overcome the embarrassment of being indiscreet and humbly he began to inquire about the artists who worked in the city. Where were they? He had seen science laboratories and gigantic factories. "Where do your painters have their workshops?" he asked. They answered that Mario Merz had died, that Michelangelo Pistoletto had gone. That if he wanted to meet them, Giulio Paolini and Nicola De Maria lived in a nearby square and others were still active. There were also some young artists but life wasn't easy for them. "Where are your poets?" They answered that Alessandro Barrico, Giuseppe Culicchia and Ernesto Ferrero wrote with great craft. "Where are the musicians, the composers, the architects?" Alberto Basso and Carlo Olmo had presented illustrious ones but there were not very many.

"Look, where is your culture factory? Who produces culture? What do you do to make it work?" His hosts were puzzled by such direct questions. They glanced at one another and said nothing.

He had been too discreet to ask the prices of the artists as they had been mentioned but he was amazed there were so few of them. So few and with so little visibility in the city – perhaps they were not well loved or well hated.

"Where are your princes and patrons?" They answered that there were no longer any, not even in Milan or Florence. Businesses and banking foundations were the new princes of culture, but they preferred to conserve the past and were afraid to back much that was new.

There were other things he did not understand, like how to pay for an admission ticket to the churches and palaces, called museums, where works of art were conserved. Finally he did not understand why people loved works of art from the past so much and contemporary artworks so little. Or not at all. Why should producing culture be less important than consuming culture produced in the dead and distant past?

Xian, China, 2007

He remembered he had had well over a thousand warriors, at least 10,000, armed, accompanied by war chariots, led by generals. Immobile guardians of his memory, sentinels of his peace, faithful sentries of the imperial tomb. He walked through the orderly ranks of the imperial legions with the proud majesty that befit the First Emperor of China. For 38 years he and his architects had overseen the building of the mausoleum. Some 700,000 artisans and over eighty excellent artists, coming from the Imperial Palace or renowned pottery workshops, had worked for his glory. Summoned from the furthest reaches of the empire, they had hammered bronze and shaped and signed terracotta statues, creating lifelike warriors, arms, chariots and well-fed horses. Seen together, the whole gave a powerful sense of the army's readiness, of motion in stillness. Color had been used to endow each solid, compact soldier with a lifelike, individualized facial expression. The statues looked as though they were waiting for the command to go into battle.

His emotion bordered on paroxysm. It seemed to him that he could recognize each of his men; despite the terracotta's solidity, its definitive rigidity, he longed to speak to his horses, hear their soft whinny. Qin Shi Huang, the First Emperor (221–210 BCE), was tired. He hid among his men near the bronze chariots until the pits closed for the day. Now that he was alone, he began to inspect his warriors. The late-afternoon light brought the legions back to life. He donned his imperial robes, sat with his generals and wept for the China that had been lost and never again found. "I have visited many prefectures," he said, "But nowhere did I see the great advances that we made live again, except in the work of young artists at Beijing's *Factory 798*. I asked the officials I met about culture in modern China. 'What great works are being made today? What has been done since the Great Wall was built and since this terracotta army, called the eighth wonder of the world, was completed? Where are the artists and artisans creating works of enduring value?'"

They told him that they had spent 300 million dollars to build the new Beijing Opera near the Imperial City, but he thought sadly that the architect was French; they were constructing the largest dam in the world, the Three Gorges, but this meant that ancient villages would be submerged. The villages would be forgotten, people would be uprooted from their land and their traditions.

He had also walked through the silk district in Hang Zhou, once famous for producing the world's most beautiful silks, but had fled, horrified by the cheap trash he had seen. Rather than quality he had found low prices and poor quality merchandise. They told him it was the price that had to be paid for globalization. He was not convinced.

"In October 2007," he added, "I heard President Hu Jintao speak at the opening of the 17th National Congress of the Chinese Communist Party. The President said, 'We must [...] vigorously develop the cultural industry, launch major projects to lead the industry as a whole, speed up the development of cultural industry bases and clusters of cultural industries with regional features, nurture key enterprises and strategic investors, create a thriving cultural market and enhance the industry's international competitiveness.' In short, we are late and backward in conserving and producing culture. You are still a living example for the future."

Thousands of miles away, Da Vinci's questions were posed once more. "Where are the artists that shape terracotta and fuse bronze? Where are your great sculptors, architects, musicians, calligraphers?" During his reign art had achieved a level of extraordinarily modern naturalness and expressiveness; beauty had been created. It was understandable that in the dynasties that followed his, new cultures had emerged and ancient ones disappeared, but why had no love of art flowered in the current generation? Then the pale light of dusk faded. Night fell.

This book is not a reply to Leonardo da Vinci's or Qin Shi Huang's musings and the questions they asked. Nor is it a nostalgic regression to an Italian Renaissance or Qin Dynasty forever finished. It is instead a reflection on the need to retie the knots that have come undone in the string of creativity that joins generations.

An exclusive club of fortunate cities are renewing the experience and models of cultural production. New York, Paris, London, Berlin and a handful of others are emblematic examples. But the world as a whole does not seem to be projecting itself towards producing culture. If, for example, we look at the Middle East, we see that an impressive accumulation of ancient culture has no corresponding contemporary production. The same can be said for many countries in Asia, Latin America, Africa and Eastern Europe. This book has in part been conceived for them, to explore how it is possible to overcome the limits of the conservation model and resist the insinuating insistence of international aid agencies that continue to propose policies that are not wholly respectful of the production of contemporary culture.

I do not intend to prefigure a new model of cultural policy, but instead wish to reconsider a model that has been abandoned. Perhaps it fell victim to the politics and globalization of markets. In the case of Italy, these markets seem bent on assigning a specialization in archaeology of culture to the country.

It is instead of utmost urgency that in Italy – and elsewhere – creativity should be encouraged to re-emerge and that the frontiers of culture, in whatever way it is manifested, be moved forward. Applying the industrial image of production to an intangible and immaterial commodity may seem to be disrespectful, given the aura that normally surrounds a work of art, but it can serve to convince us that what is at stake is a choice that is there for us to make and carry through on at any time. We just need to want to.

In the first part of this volume I discuss some aspects of the production-based model of culture, first comparing this model with the one based on conserving culture, typical of the cultural-heritage system. After this, I analyze the chain of phases and procedures that allow ideas to be produced and describe the material supports that make their distribution and consumption possible. Finally the social and environmental conditions that can increase a country's rate of creativity are explored, as creativity is a primary form of input not only for the production of culture, but also for a wide range of related cultural industries.

In the second part of the book I have chosen, albeit subjectively, a series of topics and intend to underline their strategic relevance to producing culture. Much is at stake: a nation's position in the sectors analyzed indicates whether it is succeeding or failing to move towards the economic and cultural development that can firmly establish the image of a country and its creativity as being at the center of international markets and at the heart of the knowledge society.

Part I
A Model of Production of Culture

Chapter 2
Producing Culture, Conserving Culture

It is now widely acknowledged that a country's cultural heritage is a resource for economic development. In all its forms – tangible (art, monuments, museums, libraries, archaeological finds and antiquities), intangible (music, theatre, festivals and the natural landscape) and material (the decorative arts and design) – culture is capital that can be invested to generate jobs and revenue, both in developed countries and, perhaps to an even greater extent, in developing ones.

Four Models of Cultural Policies

There are both negative and positive attitudes and approaches to culture. Thesepolicies can be classified in terms of the following four models:

- Destroying culture
- Neglecting culture
- Conserving culture
- Producing culture

Human negligence and destruction of culture, which originate in social and economic habitats or civil and religious conflicts, are negative policies, while positive policies for the conservation and production of culture, whose significance is greater, deserve more attention.

Destroying Culture

There are times when people deliberately set out to destroy works of culture or a cultural heritage itself. During wars, revolutions (Dacia Viejo 2007) and the colonialist era (Hopkirk 1980) historic cities may be sacked and plundered, museums looted and monuments destroyed. We have also witnessed the misuse of heritage sites (for example, when explosives are stored in churches or other

W. Santagata, *The Culture Factory*,
DOI 10.1007/978-3-642-13358-9_2, © Springer-Verlag Berlin Heidelberg 2010

historic buildings) or their destruction (for example, when Taliban dynamited the Bamiyan Buddhas in Afghanistan), old symbols being replaced by new ones.

The international community has been made responsible for implementing precautionary measures to ensure against the destruction of culture. To some extent, this was a response to the 1991–1995 conflict in Bosnia. Yet, although intentions may be good, getting beyond official rhetoric is difficult and most of the measures currently being taken are in post-conflict reconstruction work.

In modern cities and in many countries the destruction of culture takes the form of landscape decay. The outcome of this negative policy is generally irreversible. Re-equilibrium policies are usually costly or unfeasible.

Finally, the international competition can practice “elimination prices” as to destroy local cultural industries. Or in a more subtle way unfair competition can stifle infant industries or well established but inefficient ones such as in case of fashion, jewelry, textile or film industry. This vision however seems to belong mostly to the past than to a future more polyphonic and polycentric world.

Neglecting Culture

Although there is a great difference in terms of motivation between the deliberate destruction of culture and neglecting cultural heritage, the results of the latter can be equally devastating. This is not a new phenomenon. Throughout history there have been places and ages in which the absence of policies has been the main policy as far as the cultural heritage is concerned. The origins of this model, obviously a negative one, may lie in political ignorance, conditions of poverty, or in exploitive external domination. Some developing and poor countries are forced to neglect the economic and social value of their culture. Little money is available, other sectors are given priority and culture is ranked at the bottom of the scale.

In the early colonialist era, neglect of culture was imposed from outside. In other cases ignorance plays a part. Some countries underestimate the capital value of cultural heritage and fail to draft adequate measures to protect it. Whatever its origin, the lack of cultural policies can damage a country’s cultural heritage, sometimes irreversibly, weakening future identity and economic development.

Other examples can illustrate the negligence policy. When copyright infringements are not prosecuted and illegal markets reduced. When we assist to the decay of cultural and creative human capital. When in the gastronomic or food industry assigning too many designations of origin, or AOC in the French wine case, lowers the quality of the intellectual property signal.

Conserving Culture

When, instead, a country sees its cultural heritage as capital, that heritage needs to be valorized with appropriate policies, or it will not bear fruit – either in terms of a sense of identity and symbolic value or in economic terms. In many cases valorization has been the outcome of the revitalization of idle resources – museums not modernized, unsupervised archaeological sites, badly managed theatres. The objective contemplated in this option is the *conservation* of culture. What is at stake is a widely discussed concept, but one whose outlines are not always clear (Emiliani 1974). Conservation is an umbrella term, whose meaning, according to context, can include a variety of duties. Policies which concentrate on the past include:

1. *Safeguarding* artworks and artifacts for the public good: the century-old result of a "conservative juridical tradition, built on defining legal obligations and progressive, increasingly ample prohibitions" [ibid, 5]. Art is taken off the market and returned to the general public. The cultural heritage is protected from private interests; natural landscape is defended against a hostile building industry, against the logic of a kind of economic development which destroys the very heritage that feeds and bolsters it.
2. Defending a territory's culture from the impoverishment that occurs when there are no checks on transferring the ownership of works or preventing their irreversible disappearance (*forbidding exportation, demolition and destruction*).
3. Maintaining work in its original state (*maintenance and restoration*).
4. Adequate management and valorization of works of art.

Conservation is also a prerequisite for allowing a work of art to fulfil the important function of consolidating group-identity and to satisfy future *consumption* (visitors and cultural tourism). People see conserved culture as a collective memory, a national pride which is embedded in their country's history. The culture of the past not only is consumed as an identity good per se, but encourages the production of new culture. In other words, besides work, technology and capital, culture is a fundamental input in the production of new artistic expression.

Producing Culture

In other circumstances economic value is not extracted from physical capital accumulated over the centuries, but rather from its intangible component, particularly technique and what is called traditional knowledge. The aim of this second option is *to produce culture*. This means creating new expressions of art and culture that advance the frontiers of knowledge, whatever the field of culture, the means, technology, organization, institutions or individual or collective approach concerned is.

In essence, there are two opposing models of valorization: one oriented toward *conservation* (aesthetic, artistic or archival) and the other toward *production* (founded on the creation of new cultural and artistic expressions). The production-oriented model can be applied not only to contemporary painting, cinema, television, literature and material culture, but also to the performing arts, where directors, singers and actors add value to works as they were originally conceived, producing new culture. It can also be applied to museums, where the production of culture takes the form of adding to permanent collections and holding temporary exhibits and working for cultural decentralization and democratization of access.

In theory the two models are not equally important. Conservation is obviously subordinate to production, if only because without creation and production, future use and consumption are ruled out and safeguarding, care and valorization no longer have any meaning. The difference is enormous in monetary terms as well: in 2000 the added value of the cultural-heritage sector in Italy was estimated to be 322 million euros (Leon and Galli 2004), while for the production sector it was a total of 5,774 million euros: 319 million for the performance sectors (roughly speaking, music, theater, opera and ballet), 1,641 million for publishing, 3,483 million for television and 330 million for cinema. No matter how much we correct the data and refine methods of calculation (the significant contribution made by the visual arts is missing, for example), the production-oriented model is worth over 20 times as much as the consumption-oriented one.

And yet, on closer inspection, big cities' cultural policies show that an imperceptible bias, a *clinamen*, has overshadowed the production model, favoring the conservation-oriented one, and has turned the consuming public of tourists and visitors to art exhibitions into the arbiters who decide which strategic choices are to be made. Much more is said about the revamping of a museum's collection than about a new musical composition; statistics on visitors to exhibits of the art of the past are rattled off, emphasizing hard-earned commercial success, while little notice is taken of exhibits of contemporary visual art, a sector of dynamic importance, as sales figures for international auction houses show. The imbalance is also to be seen in growth in added value, which in the cultural-heritage sector in Italy increased by 87.1% between 1990 and 2000, when growth in the sector of cultural production was 37.4%, i.e., less than half [ibid]. The two models taken together will help us to define the concept of a country's returns on culture. Just as an activity is profitable when returns exceed costs, a country has a positive return on culture when the production of culture is greater than conservation.

Therefore the index of *profitability and cultural creativity* can be defined as the ratio between production of culture and conservation of culture (in whatever form it is expressed).

When the index goes down, it means that in relative terms a country "conserves" more that it "produces": a scenario that in the long run weakens the very content of conservation, the accumulated heritage. In a globalized world, a country that does not accumulate culture will inevitably fall behind, risking hegemony and invasion by other cultures. When the index goes up, it means instead that a country, in relative terms, is producing culture more than at least to the same extent as it is conserving it.

At different times in its history, Italy has been highly culturally creative and profitable. What is the situation today? I have a strong feeling that we are going through a phase of productive weakness. An unfortunately very rough estimate, a simple exercise done using the data (in this context more allusive than precise) given above, shows that in Italy *the index of cultural profitability and creativity* was

24.4 in 1990 and 17.9 in 2000. Although the data need to be updated and statistically refined, the negative trend in cultural production is evident.

In the long run this tendency to sacrifice production to conservation could turn out to be negative. I will explain why moving in the opposite direction is increasingly becoming a historical necessity. I wish to begin with an example taken from the museum sector. We know that many former urban industrial areas are now under-utilized or have been totally abandoned, due to recurring economic crises and structural changes, so that they are no longer needed for the purpose for which they were built. Let us imagine that a textile manufacturer that owns land decides to sell it. The city examines several possible options; it is felt that the choice should be closely linked to the site's history and local lore. Within the logic of the two models described above, the alternatives available are either to invest in cultural conservation (for example, turning the site into a traditional museum of the textile arts) or investing to produce culture (constructing a cultural center, where there would be not only a permanent collection, but also laboratories and training and study centers that would hold cultural events, exhibits and innovative productions, in an effort to dialogue with and involve the city and its social and industrial territory). The aim of both alternatives is to valorize a historically important industrial site, but in the long run, it is the second that is the better bet. Both can create jobs and generate income, but the first is located on a frontier where ideas are immobile, addressed to valorizing past achievements, while the second is on a frontier where ideas are moving toward unexplored scenarios and mobilizes the creativity of new generations.

Without underestimating how important the conservation and safeguarding of culture and the activities connected to them are in terms of image and income, I feel that after so many years spent concentrating on museums, monuments, exhibitions, and the cultural heritage, we need to return to what used to be called structural interventions, addressed to reforming countries' artistic and creative productive capacities.

The view changes radically: no longer is the emphasis on the duties involved in the safeguarding, valorization, conservation, care and fruition of the cultural heritage; instead utmost attention and assistance is made available to the chain of production whereby the value of an artwork is produced.

The supply chain, or *filière*, of art and culture is an economic concept that clearly illustrates the roles and tasks of the principal actors, public and private. Briefly, there are six phases in which a change in perspective and in institutional responsibility are apparent.

1. The first phase in the supply chain needed to produce works of art and culture is the selection of *artists and creative individuals*. Often institutional methods, from patronage to markets, public examinations and academies, are not up to meeting the international-scale, globalized challenge of the world of art and cultural industry. This phase includes education and it should be emphasized that improving the quality of schools of the fine arts, conservatories, and public and private programs (grants, awards, aid, etc.) for art and creativity is an

enormous task, one that political decision-makers fear and are only too willing to leave to others.

2. The second phase is the one in which the *creation of ideas* takes place, as art is a product that is eminently intellectual. As we will see, creativity is not an epiphany, a divine revelation, but a process that can be reproduced and transmitted to future generations. Markets are seduced by the creativity expressed in art, to the point that there has been a shift in the rules of international competition, now increasingly based on a product's technical and artistic quality rather than low production costs. In this phase the question of intellectual property rights and their enforcement in markets where commercial piracy is rife inevitably arises.
3. The *conservation phase* enters the value chain because it is a source of intermediate input. It represents a public good that makes knowledge, know-how and artistic technique accumulated in the past part of the production process. Its importance is strategic, but sometimes disregarded.
4. The *production* phase is a complex articulation of coordinated activities. Costly organizational structures (theater companies and the film industry, for example), are the means employed to communicate artists' ideas. Cultural production is typified by the systemic dimension, examples of which are to be seen in the worldwide recognition of Italy's cultural districts: its museums, material culture, historic cities.
5. The *distribution* of artworks is the fifth and most strategic phase in the chain. It has become increasingly important; together with the creative phase, it drives the entire chain which functions to create value. Entrepreneurial creativity is now more than ever exposed to the challenge of innovative distributive approaches, capable of responding to consumer preference. The distribution and management of the cultural-heritage system is a vital component of this phase.
6. The final phase is *consumption*, in which the questions of quality and widening or democratization of demand once more emerge.

The public and private sectors are currently redefining the tasks, responsibilities, and areas of cooperation involved in these five phases at a higher level, to revitalize markets and encourage individual initiative by restoring responsibility, autonomy and risk-taking in vast cultural sectors that are strategic for development.

The conservationist approach to the cultural heritage is weighed down with defects that make it difficult for innovative forces to function. When in the late 1980s with Giorgio Brosio (Brosio and Santagata 1991) and Luigi Bobbio (Bobbio 1990) I was inquiring into Italy's cultural-heritage policies, our feeling was that there had been a blameworthy historic delay compared to what was being done in France, the U.S. and U.K. We wrote:

"Faced with the needs proceeding from the extraordinary number of cultural, historic and artistic works the country possesses and the state of conservation they are in, although Italy's financial and organizational commitment is one of the highest in Europe, it is still not adequate. Nevertheless, to introduce a positive note, the birth of the modern museum – an efficiently managed major cultural operator and conveyor of an aesthetic project – is no longer only a dream: Turin's renovated Egyptian Museum, Milan's Brera, Città degli Uffizi in Florence, and others are overcoming resistance and myriad difficulties and rising to the challenge." (Brosio and Santagata 1991, 216).

Unfortunately the conservationist approach to cultural heritage turned into a watered-down version of the original expectations even before achieving the results dreamt of some 15 years ago. The list of its defects is long and cruel: it subverts the order of priorities in terms of producing art and culture; it concentrates on valorizing the past per se; it is intrinsically conservative. It is a political-cultural lobby: the more decentralized the system, the more conservation is prey to local political machines; the more centralized the system, the further it is from citizens' preferences. Finally, it represents a closed cultural model – museum-dominated and institutionalized.

In addition, the conservationist approach is weak because it creates synergy with very few economic sectors or parts of these sectors. I am referring above all to tourism, small restoring and building firms, information technology companies specializing in cataloguing, specialist publishers, and little else. These are strong links in a weak social fabric. And it is obsolete because consumer habits have changed and the consumer now plays an increasingly active overall role in the cultural industries, a role I would call productive. Consumer interpretation plays a part in artistic creation. Consumer and artist are linked in a single creative experience (Mossetto 1993).

The systemic value of producing culture is far different. By training and selecting artists, designers and other creatives, it can improve a country's job market on all fronts and upgrade its most strategic sector, the one Florida called the creative class (Florida 2002). In the widest sense, this includes engineers and scientists, as well as people working in the fields of architecture and design, education, the arts, music and entertainment, whose economic function is to create new ideas [ibid, 8]. The creative class also includes professionals and managers that apply creativity to the functioning and development of economic organizations and companies.

When new ideas are conceived and put into practice, the production of culture is extended to productive activities undergoing enormous growth throughout the world. According to available estimates (Howkins 2001), the total creative industry worldwide was worth 2,240 billion dollars in 1999. The figure is astronomical, given that it is one and a half times Italy's gross national product for 2004 and nearly twice the GNP of all the countries in the Middle East and Africa together (1,144 billion dollars in 2004). Recent data on the cultural and creative sectors in Europe reveal a turnover of over 654 billion euros, equal to 2.6% of Europe's GNP in 2003. In 2004, the sector employed approximately 5.8 million workers, 3.1% of the active workforce (KEA European Affairs 2006).

The way the sector is defined has also undergone profound change. The traditional divisions into visual arts, performing arts and the cultural heritage (landscape, museums, monuments) have now been joined by productive industrial activity: creative companies (principally those involved in intellectual property rights) and culture-based service industries (e.g., tourism, professional training, legal services, advertising and the entire sector which reproduces sound, texts or images with digital means.

Producing culture is therefore an economic activity. In the era of the knowledge society and global markets it is once again a pioneering one and is becoming increasingly complex as it is adapted to a far wider range of goods and services, both in terms of content and technology, and to a heterogeneous public. What, for example, do a painting, an opera and a television series have in common? Far more than is commonly thought.

In the next chapter, retracing the past on a path along which we will re-encounter artists and the ideas they expressed and disseminated, as well as an immense nation of consumers and lovers of culture, it will be possible to examine the links in a chain that miraculously lives again for each new cultural product and is reborn with each new generation of creative talent.

Chapter 3
The Supply Chain of Cultural Production

Although there are profound differences between the cultural heritage and artistic heritage, the two share certain fundamental economic characteristics, have similar strong ties with the market and are subject to the same institutional rules. A single analytical frame of a supply chain of processes that produce culture can therefore be applied to both without oversimplifying or trivializing what is involved.

As was pointed out, the chain develops in six phases – selection, conception/creation, production, conservation, distribution and consumption. They succeed one another, expanding or shrinking according to circumstances, in a process capable of continual regeneration. Many of the questions pertinent to individual phases will be dealt with in detail in the chapters that follow. Here the reader will find an overview of the process.

The First Phase: Selecting Artists

Obviously the first step in any production process is to ensure the availability of the agents and factors on which production depends. In the purest form of artistic production, capital and labor are incorporated in the same person and the first problem that needs to be faced is how to go about *selecting artists*, in other words how to discover creative talent. Nature bestows artistic intelligence randomly, hence there needs to be specific intervention to recognize talented individuals, as every non-valorized talent corresponds to a net social loss. Put as simply as possible, if Giotto had been a shepherd instead of a painter and architect, Florence, Naples, Padua and all of Italy would now be without the masterpieces he created.

Market-Driven Selection Processes

In the modern world the selection of artists by market forces represents the most powerful means of choice wielded by producers, consumers, lovers and collectors of art. As will be seen, the market chooses the artists preferred by the public,

W. Santagata, *The Culture Factory*,
DOI 10.1007/978-3-642-13358-9_3, © Springer-Verlag Berlin Heidelberg 2010

granting them copyright protection and remunerating them with royalties and direct payment. In this respect it should be noted that if artists' attitude towards their work were that of *art for art's sake*, as is often imagined, there would be no need for an art market – it would have no role to play. In reality people become artists for a complex set of reasons: the joy of creating; to seek fame, and (in part and for some artists) for economic reward. Substantially, market logic is articulated in expressing consumers' and art collectors' preferences. They are the ones, through the payment of the price asked (e.g., for a painting), or contractual remuneration or royalties (in many other cases), who can provide economic support for artists and, indirectly, determine which artists will be successful, and which ones will not survive.

In other sectors, instead, it is an entrepreneur's investment that is the decisive factor. When filmmakers or theater impresarios select artists whose works they feel will give them a return on their initial investment, they play a crucial role in determining success.

The market and its industrial institutions can also function as a selective factor in another way: through on-the-job training, in other words learning by doing. The workshops of Renaissance Florence no longer exist, but in the context of many of Italy's cultural districts (in fashion and the production of material culture in general), tacit knowledge, hands-on training and learning through direct observation and experience continue to function as efficient systems of selection.

Non-Market Selection Processes

Non-market selection mechanisms are equally important. In what follows I will briefly describe public action, patronage, self-selection and political selection.

1. *The state*. Selection takes place through the school system and public examinations that allocate grants, positions and opportunities, in theory to the most deserving, most talented artists. Art education throughout the world is undergoing reform: art institutes and secondary schools, academies for the fine arts, conservatories and vocational high schools for the industrial arts are adopting new methods in order to catch up with the best-known U.S. and U.K. schools of art and design.
2. *Patronage*. With this method of selection, the paternalistic preferences of a small number of wealthy individuals are imposed at the collective, social level. Patrons' choices are private, made without interference of any sort, and as such may be inadequate to the needs of the society in which they are operating. When the patron is a non-profit organization, for example a banking foundation, the private component is not as strong, but the likelihood of foundations being exposed to fluctuations in the economy and finding themselves in financial difficulties in a recession can have a negative effect.
3. *Self-selection*. The self-selection process and selection based on political criteria are less conventional mechanisms. The first is an interesting case of information

economics and rational decision-making processes. It is a metaphor for reality, one that is rich in ideas and lessons (Gay 1998).

The starting point is the costs and contradictions involved in the process of selecting artists. In fact if the reference population is small, the cost of gathering the information needed to compare pairs of candidates and select the best will be low. Unfortunately, if the group is very small, the probability of identifying talent risks being excessively low and the vitality of the artistic discipline may be compromised. Conversely, it can be said that starting with a large reference population increases the number of comparisons that need to be made, and hence the information costs involved, but makes for a larger number of talented artists from which to choose the best. The dilemma, therefore, is whether it is preferable to keep costs down or face higher expenses and ensure a better chance of selecting truly talented individuals.

Analyzing the possible ways of cutting information costs, Gay concentrates on selecting artists through art academies, whose definitive function would be to signal the quality of their members. He argues that if academies were ranked in order of quality, each artist would find – and would be welcomed by – those academies where s/he was qualified to work, because the personal costs involved in belonging to a wrong academy would be so high that the artist would be induced to choose a different one. For example, a highly talented artist would not adapt to a mediocre academy, but move to a better one or found a new one; a mediocre artist, challenged by colleagues whose quality s/he could never hope to match, would move to a lower-level academy. The advantage of self-selection would consist in the fact that we would no longer need to collect information on individual artists but would only need to know which academy the artist came from, as different academies would correspond to different degrees of talent.

4. *Political selection*. The selection mechanism I am about to describe is typical of systems of political patronage, where relationships are conceived in terms of being either a friend or an enemy. Politics with its modern territorial divisions – at the city, provincial and regional and nationwide levels – is a world of special allocations. In fact representative political systems' decisional processes can take the place of the pricing system in allocative selection when politicians intervene in the world of art with methods Hayek would have disdained as tribal, typical of *the Rule of Men*, the antithesis of the incorruptible *Rule of Law*.

The art field in a given area is crossed by axes that divide it into its components; they are magnetic axes that attract and polarize groups of artists seeking affirmation and success. One of the principal axes observed in a study of young artists in Turin in the late 1980s (Santagata 1998a) was the one that set state and market in opposition, i.e. at one pole artists who conceive of art as a means of social criticism, at the other, artists who consider art an expression of a private, individual, unconscious world. The state-oriented artists seek to establish a strong relation between politics and culture; the market-oriented ones are fully exposed to the rules of competition. The former work with the chairs of the city council's culture committees, foundations and museums. They eschew risk and are selected by politicians with public funds to spend. The latter work with private galleries and, like gallery owners, run the risk of failure. The artists whose works are allocated by the political system and within it must satisfy or at least be in sympathy with the preferences of those in power; the others respond to the preferences of collectors and the public.

Although the characteristics of the two poles have been exaggerated, there is no denying the fact that in the art world, politically protected islands of allocation have survived: artists who do not sell but whose work is promoted, who exhibit in public institutional spaces, who win competitions, whose works are hung on the walls of city and regional offices, if not in local museums. Here the symbolic dimension is leveled by the political dimension, often renouncing and at times losing its universal significance.

The Second and Third Phases: Conception and Production of a Work of Art

While working, artists first devote themselves to the production of ideas. On closer examination, however, in the creative act, there come together, often indissolubly, two successive phases of the process of cultural production: the *conception* of the work of art and its *production*.

On the level of *conception*, a phenomenon which is at the same time instinctive, intuitive and logical, the work of art is merely an idea or, according to Gide, the exaggeration of an idea: an innovative act that is unique, exalted, meditated and can be either individual or collective, a set of messages capable of arousing emotion and sensations in those who create or consume. This first creative moment, however, is not in itself complete, as the work of art only acquires a definitive form during the subsequent phase of *production*. What a distance there is from the original intuition and the finished novel, film or symphony! In the visual and plastic arts, moreover, the phases of conception and production coincide, and only when indissolubly united do they allow the work of art to take shape. The painter's idea has life and form only at the moment when it is transformed into drawing, color and shapes on canvas.

What is more, an idea – poem, melody, pictorial composition, design – *must* be produced not only to fulfill its promise and be realized, but also so that it can be revealed to others. To be enjoyed, art in fact must be translated into, or fixed, in a *medium*. This may be a material one – book, CD, canvas, stone, film – or immaterial one – symphonic concert, theater performance, the outcome of a combination of organizational activities and productive factors. In this case the work can be enriched and completed by another artistic figure, an *interpreter*. This is typically the case in a performance, where the orchestra conductor, singers or actors are considered artists because their work adds something to the original idea. For a book, instead, giving form to literary creation does not normally require the mediation of an interpreter (although a translator may sometimes be needed).

The connection between original idea, its production, and the medium through which it is conveyed by its creator to others varies depending on the art form being considered. For most forms of art, the support has no other function than to transmit the original idea in a given medium, e.g. a painting, CD, film, book or concert. In other cases, the support has been created to be used for a specific purpose, e.g. a church, palace, salt cellar, carpet. Defining a church an art object means that we see it not only as serving a specific function as a place of worship, but also as having aesthetic properties capable of arousing artistic feelings. Seen in this way, all products made by human beings and those existing in nature can be perceived in very different ways: they can be objects of artistic or social perception or may simply be considered everyday, domestic consumer items.

It is therefore the creator's and observer's *aesthetic intention* that determines that an object is not a purely functional one. Aesthetic intention makes it possible for an object – a Ferrari car, for example – to be appreciated both for its *function*, in line with its producer's original intention, and for its *form*, in line with the intention of those who look at it (Panofsky 1939).

For the creative phase, the question that is most delicate point and as we will see, most ambiguous, is the safeguarding of intellectual property rights. There are contradictions in the legal recourses defined in *common law* and in *civil law*, even discrimination between different kinds of creators. The ideas of painters, composers, writers and directors are subject to different safeguards in terms of efficacy and the extent of protection the law envisions. An additional problem is that illegal markets and criminal counterfeiters (of which more will be said in the following chapters) have become a permanent threat to the system for safeguarding intellectual property rights.

The creation of a work of art was *par excellence* an individual act, with partial exceptions, mainly in the figurative and plastic arts. Today examples of teamwork are common: music scores for films, teams of writers that put together best sellers. In addition, the production phase often requires the presence of a complementary organization, for example a theater company, an orchestra, a museum.

A wide range of enterprises are present in the art world, from private, profit-making companies, to cooperatives, to non-profit organizations, to public bodies. This variety is in large measure an outcome of economic convenience. The arts enrich some creators, interpreters and cultural industries, yet they can be unprofitable or even cause financial catastrophes. For reasons associated with ineluctably rising costs – Baumol's controversial theory of "cost disease" (Baumol and Bowen 1966) – the production of many artistic services, e.g. a theater performance, opera or classical music concert – may produce little profit, or even run at a loss. As a result, in almost all countries, artistic services are heavily subsidized by the government. Without this help, we would certainly see far less of many forms of art, if they did not disappear altogether.

Nor is there any guarantee that the production of goods – a book, painting, CD or video – will produce a profit. Precisely because each artistic product is an original and to receive attention it must be distinctive, prior experience counts little and economic outcome contains a high margin of risk.

Finally, in sectors that produce material culture – art glass, ceramics, designer furnishings, textiles, fashion, musical instruments – there is a strong tendency towards industrial agglomeration, in other words, the formation of cultural districts, places for integrated production involving micro, small and middle-sized firms. This formula, of great interest for the theory of sustainable local economic development, will be the subject of a chapter of its own, as it has been one of Italy's most original contributions to the theory and practice of economic development.

No analysis of the production phase can be complete if the recent advances in Information and Communication Technologies (ICTs) are not taken into account. Their extraordinary impact on the distinction between production and consumption is so strong as to blur the distinction itself. The phenomena of the *prosumers* and user-generated content illustrate this point.

Prosumer, a neologism conjugating the word producer (or professional) with the word consumer, was coined by Alvin Toffler in the book *The Third Wave* (Toffler 1980). New technologies make it possible for the consumer to assume an active role as co-innovator, or music composer or media co-author. The more involved in the production process consumers become, the more they can add something new and creative to the work of art they are consuming.

User-generated content refers mainly to media content produced by an end-user. Although being part of a virtual community on the web is not a specific consumer choice, it implies the production of some new content. The main applications in which user-generated content can be found include question-answer databases, discussion boards, social networking sites, mobile phones and videos, podcasting, and video games, where the essential parts of the game are created by the players themselves. As the media companies have realized that users can produce interesting materials, they have adjusted their business models accordingly.

Prosumers and *user-generated contents* have modified and short-circuited the value chain of cultural production. This is one of the most recent examples of how new technologies that are accessible and affordable to the general public can change traditional ways of thinking about the production of culture.

The Fourth Phase: Conservation

As was shown in the previous chapter, the link in the chain of creating value whose importance is comparable to production is the conservation of art and the cultural and natural heritage. Without going over ground that has already been covered, I wish to add some further comments on the topic.

It is important to consider that conservation creates employment in a sophisticated sector, given, first, the qualifications and skills restorers and those working in the construction industries need to have, and secondly the innovative techniques and avant-garde technology used to treat materials and artifacts. If a painting has been made using both sides of a canvas, it can now be divided in two; micro-organisms can be used to protect and reinforce stone; archeometrics is an important tool in exploring archaeological sites; X-rays, sonograms and automata allow us to see ambient details that would be invisible to the naked eye.

In the conservation sector we find both small, traditional firms and technologically advanced multinationals. Given their nature, conservation activities are for the most part financed with public funds or by non-profit organizations whose justification can be traced to the non-exclusive nature of their consumption.

The Fifth Phase: Distribution

Every creation is born from an original idea that is given form and made available to others via *methods of distribution* specific to each sector of the arts; there can be more than one method in a given sector. This is the fourth phase in the chain: a play can be distributed by being performed in a theater, a monument by being shown to the public. Methods of distribution can, however, be simultaneous and varied: in fact an opera can be given a live performance in a theatre or can be filmed and shown in a cinema, broadcast on television or sold as a DVD for home viewing. A painting can be exhibited in a museum or acquired by a private collector.

For certain cultural items, say churches, or artistic monuments and buildings that are truly collective consumer goods – the phases of realization and distribution coincide.

In addition, the choice of means of distribution can influence how a work is produced. Let me explain. When the decision is made to distribute an artistic product cinematographically rather than as a stage play, the technology and expressive means employed are sufficiently different to make for qualitatively different products.

Distribution is the phase closest to final consumer preference. Given new patterns of consumption, it may now be the economically and strategically most important phase in the supply chain of cultural production. Distribution conditions creation and the productive phase; it makes it possible to expand into new markets; ultimately it is the phase that is most receptive to new networking technologies and the IT revolution.

The Sixth Phase: Consumption

The fifth phase is that of *enjoyment* of the work of art, by consumers (the general public), whose principal constraint is lack of time, and by collectors, whose principal constraint is lack of capital.

The consumption of art requires the combination of two elements: works of art and consumers' time. The same thing happens, it is true, for any other good, but in the case of the arts there are substantive technical reasons why the time spent cannot be reduced. To make the idea clearer, let us use the example of a Mozart composition for string quartet. Today, as two centuries ago, four interpreters and 30 min of listening time are needed, whatever medium is used to produce it: recording or live performance. Such instances occur in sectors which are technologically stagnant, where there is no increase in productivity either in production or in consumption. The outcome is paradoxical. As a society gradually becomes richer, time costs more (losing an hour of work means sacrificing a higher hourly wage). If we then take into account that consuming itself takes time, the richer we become, the less leisure time we have. This is a very different view from the one that saw economic progress leading to increased free time, which failed to take into account that consuming culture does not take place instantaneously, outside time.

There is thus a sort of contradiction in the evolution of the consumption of art, or rather increased wealth and higher educational levels, which create the need for ever new cultural experiences, have two contrasting effects: people want and can afford more goods but have less time to consume them.

The importance of this is twofold. As increasing the amount of time individuals have to dedicate to culture is not an option, in order to augment the total consumption of art, we need to encourage new cohorts of consumers to appreciate artistic expression and see this as a pleasurable experience. There is, however, a limited number of ways in which this can be done. First, investment in human capital can be increased, using the educational system to create the conditions needed for more intense and more widespread consumption of culture. Secondly, the physical part of art products can be acted upon by fostering techniques that cut the time it takes to access them. The second method is the cultural industry's response to consumers' lack of time. The trend is for goods to take the place of services and is occurring in ever more varied and vast cultural sectors. Enormous strides were made in the twentieth century, when the discovery of radio waves revolutionized long-distance transmission and reproduction techniques made it possible to discern the potential in recording and storing sounds for future consumption, independently from the space-time context in which they were originally produced.

We have entered an age in which culture and art are ubiquitous. Technology has altered the ways culture can be reproduced and transmitted, setting in motion an alluring, as yet unfinished process: home consumption and nearly total convergence of supports.

In the age of castles and courts, having culture brought to you was a privilege enjoyed by kings and nobles. Music and theater performances were an integral part of courtesans' days and were regulated by formal etiquette and representative of hierarchies of power.

With the birth of the modern state and changes in technology and the cost of traditional activities, orchestras, painters and acting companies slowly abandoned the royal courts, theaters and chapels, as a life of pomp and princely prestige became increasingly difficult to maintain. Art, music and theater, became urban, bourgeois phenomena – in forms we would now call public and collective. The transformation reached its height in the nineteenth century. The nobility was no longer able to afford its former sumptuous, ostentatious lifestyle and the emerging bourgeoisie became the public to which art was addressed, widening its base and transforming it into popular consumption. Going to the theater, a concert or an art exhibit became a bourgeois rite and new forms of organization emerged to make this development possible.

The popularity of certain genres, especially opera, operetta, plays and French boulevard theater, was at its height between the late-nineteenth and early-twentieth centuries, when cultural consumption at home first appeared as an alternative to live consumption. The first art to be affected was music. New technology made it possible to have access to musical consumption in less time and at a lower cost.

In the space of a few decades, better quality sound reproduction meant that listening to music at home could equal hearing a live performance and people opted to acquire goods – records and radios – rather than services. Consuming culture at home slowly gained in prestige.

A similar process was taking place in the field of the figurative arts. First prints and then photography made it possible to conserve and reproduce original images. The invention of television and today's digital image-transmission over international telecommunications networks has exponentially sped up at-home consumption of images and sounds.

At-home consumption has many advantages. The list that follows is not in order of importance but is indicative of a well-delineated typology. Emphasis is on the fact that at-home consumption can eliminate the sense of fatigue that assails the museum visitor. The pleasure of contemplating works one at a time is greater: we all know the ear cannot listen to ten different symphonies at the same time, yet in a museum our eyes are expected to take in hundreds of paintings. Our intelligence, aesthetic pleasure and emotions are dulled by seeing too many works, too densely exhibited.

The contradiction between the time – generally long – employed by its creator to produce a work and the time – generally brief – employed in its consumption can be reduced. I am referring to the possibility of producing virtual, on-line reconstructions of paintings. Someone who gives a painting a hurried glance loses the sense of the artist's difficult, halting journey, the sense of process, and enjoys only the end product. Moreover, with modern visual-reproduction techniques it is possible to examine a painting in greater detail and grasp particulars that might go unnoticed during a museum visit.

In one's own home one is not tied to a date, to opening and closing times. Being able to choose the moment of consumption means one is consuming art when one's spirit is most receptive, in a climate that differs little from the one in which the work was created. At-home consumption, finally, lowers the costs of access to artworks – the money and time spent on transportation, ritual costs ("proper" attire, having to walk down long museum corridors) – increasing opportunities for consumption.

Of course there are also disadvantages. Basically they are those connected to the transmission of works of art by mechanical and electronic means. Although there has been great technological progress in transmitting and reproducing sounds and images, there is a risk of weakening direct aesthetic emotion, of losing the effect of context. By and large, however, the public seems to be satisfied with the new goods being offered, even though for some people art consumption in the private dimension represents a weakening of the social and symbolic components potentially present in the act of consuming culture.

The emergence of at-home consumption of art was made possible by the new technologies that enabled us to modify the physical part of an artwork. Historically this happened in two complementary directions: that of diffusion and that of conservation and reproduction.

In recent decades new categories of goods have replaced – obviously without eliminating them, but by changing the sense they have – the services offered by cultural providers: thus the stereo and CD have taken the place of the live concert. What distinguishes the items in question is that they can be used again and again, furnishing a series of private services. Television, the CD or video/DVD reader are now far more relevant to people's lives than the services they correspond to (a film, music, a TV series), as is true of cars and household appliances in comparison to public transport and household help.

Where once we acquired final services, we now acquire goods. One reason is the change in *relative cost*. The costs for services, say for a live theater performance, have grown far more than those for goods – favored by a rapid evolution in technology and significant increase in productivity. Rational consumers therefore acquire goods and they themselves reproduce, albeit less professionally, the same services they previously consumed live. On the other hand, not only has technological progress lowered production costs, it has also enormously increased the quality of goods, increasing the likelihood that consumers will acquire goods rather than services. With the movie projector having been replaced by the DVD reader and the phonograph by the CD player, the acquisition of goods rather than final services is increasingly likely. The explanation for this process is that goods and the autonomous consumption they make possible ensure a *time savings*, the result of eliminating the time spent traveling to public exhibition/performance sites.

Today the two functions of distribution and reproduction are united in a sole technological medium, internet, that makes it possible to reach the final consumer at home. It is the convergence of a cultural offer in a single support: internet and the PC with its monitor and sound system, their natural terminal.

The strategy of replacing services with goods has been an original response to consumers' lack of time, but an equally important development has been an exponential increase in the demand for information. The globalization of markets, developments in telematics and in networking require that immense information resources be available at a low cost. Technology has provided an answer – the IT revolution, a perfect example of the principles described in Moore's law: since the 1950s the price of the basic element of the revolution, the microchip, has gone down 50% every 18 months!

Art products, finally, are used not only for consumer activities, but also as investments. This is especially true of the figurative arts, which produce material goods, therefore ones that can be stored, whose value can increase in time, making for a more complex scenario. Not only do we have consumers on one side and artists/producers on the other, but also investors, speculators and specialized intermediaries.

The process of artistic reproduction evolves and is reiterated, accompanied by continuous tension between choices made by the market, where everything has a price and there are no free lunches, and non-market ones, which via public intervention and forms of patronage, are better able to safeguard certain values.

Corresponding to the various phases of development in the chain of production, a variety of collateral markets have taken shape (the art market, theater performances, concerts, interpreters, superstars, etc.) where the encounter between demand and supply generates situations – for example large profits or large losses – that inevitably influence the correct functioning of the entire process.

It can be seen, even in this rapid description, that the model of production of art is of great importance. Culture is taking back its fundamental role in all spheres of human activity: social, intellectual and economic. Given this, we now need to turn our attention to the production of creativity, a strategic factor in the chain of processes which produce the value of works of art.

Chapter 4
Creativity as a Resource, Emotions as a Prerequisite

In modern knowledge society, the only thing we know for certain about markets is that they are completely uncertain. Technologies are born and die in rapid succession; competition is becoming ever more aggressive; products age and quickly become obsolete. Surviving in such markets depends on "staying ahead," having the capacity to untiringly create new knowledge. Creativity is thus an essential resource, the basis of innovation, of new knowledge and culture.

The model is a simple one: to produce culture and knowledge, creativity is needed, otherwise what is repetitive, academic and old hat would prevail; what is needed to produce creativity is the capacity to generate and perceive appropriate emotions, those capable of opening channels of communication with the world and conveying feelings, motivation, creative inference, a sense of discovery and risk. In other words, while science on its own is not able to reproduce a creative idea, it has nevertheless explored the environmental and social conditions that facilitate the birth and spread of such ideas and argued that emotions constitute the connection between environment and mind.

Creativity has thus become a fundamental resource in postmodern society, which demands increased input of intellectual capital to meet the challenge not only of the knowledge society, but also of what has been called the trend towards *dematerializing* products, i.e. the depreciation of their material elements in comparison to the worth of the intellectual and creative component they contain.

The approach adopted in this chapter is a deliberately limited one. There is no lack of excellent presentations on the subject and here I wish simply to go over and reconsider, from an economic viewpoint, some of the contributions which illustrate the general conditions needed for the production of creativity: how it is produced and whether it is possible to produce it; how a high general level of creativity can be maintained or, expressed differently, how creativity can be transmitted to future generations.

We can define two approaches to analyzing creativity:

- *Objective* analysis sees the creativity incorporated in an object as different from the creativity incorporated in a logical, organizational or productive process.

W. Santagata, *The Culture Factory*,
DOI 10.1007/978-3-642-13358-9_4, © Springer-Verlag Berlin Heidelberg 2010

The former refers to the concept of aesthetics or design, for example a painting or couturier clothing, the latter to the creation of a reproducible process, for example organizational flexibility in an industrial district.

- *Subjective* analysis instead sees creativity as an individual human attribute.

With little agreement on how the concept of creativity should be defined, different cognitive approaches developed, starting in the late nineteenth century. Some attempt to measure creativity in terms of economic value and use the term *creative economy* for all creative industries and services, from "content industries" (Howkins 2001), to software and design. Others analyze it through its interaction with the labor market and urban social structure (Florida 2002): who are creative workers; what is their world like; what are the laws of their markets? Yet others consider the cognitive and psychological aspects of creativity (Legrenzi 2005), investigate its relation to the economics of art and culture (Bryant and Throsby 2006), its relation to linguistic processes (Chomsky 1968), or to the mechanisms of creative inferential learning (Boden 1991).

Finally, there were those who attempted to define the intellectual and psychological attributes of genius by studying the extraordinary, dramatic lives of great artists (Kris and Kurz 1934). Creative individuals seem to be more likely to suffer from manic-depressive syndrome (Jameson 1984), guilt feelings and madness and be independent, willing to risk, and anti-conformist. In this view, the creative process of a genius seems to correspond to the rather snobbish vision of Picasso who declared, "I do not seek. I find."

From the economic point of view, creativity is a leap into the blue, a venture without limits, an anti-utilitarian commodity. It functions as a factor in self-actualization and is rich in intrinsic satisfaction. The hypothesis which sees working time merely as a production cost becomes less and less valid, the closer one approaches the sphere of creative production (Horvath 1999; Throsby 2000). Creative individuals offer others their work because this affords them pleasure. The quality of their lives depends not only on consumption but also on the possibility of choosing a creative occupation: "The desire for creativity is one of the most important motivations of human beings in general, and in our post-industrial era in particular" (Horvath 1999).

Creativity as Process

It has been said that creativity is a mental process, "the process by which the mind transforms information into combinations of concepts and produces new ideas" (Goleman 1997). Seen by the mathematician Henri Poincaré, creativity is uniting existing elements with new, hopefully useful connections. We could add that creativity is an act of the human brain that takes shape in a process that helps us think and solve problems in a way that can be considered creative.

There are two possible ways a problem can be solved: with a creative act, what in Gestalt psychology is called an insight or, according to behavioral psychologists in the United States, through the process of trial and error (Legrenzi 2005). Both approaches can be influenced by the social and environmental conditions of the external world. This means, as we will see, that it is important to perceive the messages that arrive from one's surroundings, to have open channels of communication: it is emotions that allow this to happen.

Herbert Simon's research, like studies conducted by other cognitive scientists, focused on the qualities someone needs to have to be creative. For Simon creativity consists in having good problem-solving abilities: "Acts are judged to be creative when they produce something that is novel and that is thought to have social value. Interesting or valuable novelty is the touchstone of the creative" (Simon 1986).

According to Simon, the process that leads to creativity, and assumes the existence of a purpose, is based on three conditions:

1. *Preparation.* "'Chance,' in the words of Pasteur, 'favors the prepared mind'. A casual discovery per se does not exist. It is surprise, the departure from the expected, that creates the fruitful accident; and there are no surprises without expectations, nor expectations without knowledge" [ibid].
2. *Expertise.* No-one – fashion designer, chess player, composer – can achieve excellence without "an intensive effort to acquire knowledge and skill in a domain of expertise" [ibid]. Scholars generally agree that creativity is manifested in a specific domain and that only Leonardo da Vinci and a handful of others were creative in two or three different domains (Amabile and Tighe 1993).
3. *Risk taking.* Scientific research often involves accepting calculated risks. "Information is only valuable if others do not have it or do not believe it strongly enough to act on it. [...] Science is an occupation for gamblers". We must take risks if we wish to explore new fields in a creative way, because generic information provides no differential advantage: "Scientists require a 'contrarian' streak that gives them the confidence to pit their knowledge and judgment against the common wisdom of their colleagues" (Simon 1986).

I would add *tenacity* to being prepared, experienced and willing to take risks because often the creative solution is not just around the corner, and can be reached only by those with the stamina to "keep on keeping on."

The *problem-solving* model does not reveal what the biological and physical sources of creativity are, how it is produced by the human brain. It points to certain conditions, which could be called personal and individual, that favor creative problem solving. To complete the picture, considering that environmental and social influences are equally important, it is useful to analyze the remarkable discoveries made by Antonio Damasio (1994) concerning the relationship between mind, brain, emotions and behavior.

Mind and Brain, Body and Emotions

The body counts, the brain counts. Damasio's message is that in order to reason we need our body: "The body is the basic reference for the mental processes." Body and brain both play fundamental roles in the thought process, particularly in decision making, problem solving and creativity: they are responsible for processing the emotions that originate when we interact with the external world and constantly affect us. Body and brain, as a single organism, preside over the interaction between the individual and the environment, which is itself to some extent the product of human activity.

The emotions count. Emotions or emotional experiences are defined by Damasio as "...the series of changes which occur in the body and the brain, generally in reaction to specific mental content" [ibid]. When dealing with emotions, approaches and definitions differ. For example, according to Elster, "Emotions, like beliefs and desires, can be defined either as occurrent mental events, or as dispositions for such events to occur." What is of interest to us in this definition is that while emotions are largely beyond the brain's control, dispositions can be consciously and amply modeled (Elster 1996).

One of the most remarkable discoveries in modern neurobiology was locating the area in the brain responsible for producing an emotional state in the body. The story, many of whose facets are truly extraordinary, of Phineas Gage (1823–1860) recounts what happened to a railway foreman who had an accident while doing construction work and suffered injury to the prefrontal area of his brain. Gage was left without any apparent physical injury, but ended his life alone, incapable of communicating with others, in the Barnum and Bailey Circus where he play acted being himself. What had happened? Further clinical and experimental studies seem to show that the brain's prefrontal cortex is the center of emotion recognition and in its absence the body is only capable of having "knowledge without emotions." Damasio establishes that the reasoning of individuals who lack emotions develops normally, but is blocked by their inability to decide. Their reasoning proceeds as an infinite sequence of comparisons between the costs and benefits inherent in alternative actions, without their ever being able to reach a final decision. Rationality without emotions is shown to be a process without an end. *Pure* rationality spells failure for decisional processes.

Damasio believes the decisional process becomes possible when what he calls *somatic markers* (a sort of somatic disposition) are present, images which emerge from the emotions and act on the brain's neural structures, enabling it to understand that it is necessary to end a reasoning process (which is leading nowhere) and choose between the available alternatives.

Damasio recognizes that the power of reason and experiencing emotions grow together. He establishes a correlation but not a cause-and-effect nexus. Nevertheless, if Damasio's conjecture is correct, the emotions constitute a real contribution to the rational process and their "production" is a prerequisite for the development of creativity.

Emotions Count, the Environment Counts

Without emotions we cannot log in to the natural and social environments. This is the physical–mechanical prerequisite for creativity. By producing good emotions we can educate for creativity and innovation; by producing bad ones, for scholastic repetitiveness. Much depends on the quality of the environment and its collective dimension.

Creativity as a problem-solving activity depends on the capacity to interact with a continuous flow of emotions. Good emotions influence us positively if we live in an environment where they abound: an environment where there are no intellectual limitations and ideas can circulate freely, an environment where there is freedom to associate ideas and to experiment. The theory of emotions explains why, if we wish to stimulate creativity, we need to rethink and reorganize what could be called the organizational and mental environment, including the one generally found in businesses.

According to recent sociological studies in the United States (Florida 2002), it is important to discover which conditions are needed for creatively rich environments to exist and the most creative environments are those in which there are the highest levels of technology, talent and tolerance. Tolerance in particular helps explain why creative spirits are attracted to a place or city.

Italy's economic experience seems to show that cultural districts are particularly creative environments in which good emotions, tacit knowledge, and ultimately, a wealth of creative stimuli are produced.

Body and brain interact with nature; they are immersed in a universe of relationships, emotions and connections. It is safe to say that without social relationships and the emotions they involve, it is not possible to have a rational approach to problem solving or to be creative. Rephrased, that means that modifying the productive or research environment so that it expresses creative emotions is the key factor in producing, increasing and transmitting creativity.

We need to shift the center of analysis. We are not yet in a position to fully understand the workings of the neural mechanisms that produce creativity, so the problem is not how creativity should be taught, what the best methods to adopt would be. We do, however, know enough to produce creativity by developing suitable environments. If for now it is unrealistic to think of reproducing an individual creative act, it *is* possible to develop a social and educational environment favorable to the generation of creative acts. There are things we can do to create creative environments.

As we will see in the chapters that follow, art academies, professional schools and the education sector in general are the first environments that can generate the conditions which could stimulate the development of creativity. After them come all forms of in-service training, from apprenticeships to the transmission of tacit knowledge to work–study programs. In this sense, creativity is a key facet of human capital, along with the traditional factors of which it is composed. This means that investing in the factors that increase human capital (knowledge, style, personality, motivation) will lead to an increase in the rate of creativity in a society.

Creativity is a non-exhaustible and non-saturable commodity. The ideas produced by human creativity are fully exploitable, but not exhaustible. The creativity that goes into fashion products, for example, is connected to social evolution and is thus constantly moving forward and being renewed. Design is linked to its times, and hence is always different. Industry in this case finds an inexhaustible source of intellectual resources, which represent a new arena for encounter and competition between companies.

But it is especially in the industrial atmosphere of micro and small firms aggregated in industrial districts that we can breathe creativity. As we will see, however, the evolution of creativity is not straightforward: alternating periods of great creativity and phases of stagnation are typical of all artistic sectors and in many cases, also of cultural districts. Institutions have new responsibilities and must employ new means, such as extending intellectual property rights, to enable us to produce culture by means of creativity.

Beyond the mystery of the production of creativity, other strategic issues should be discussed. Is creativity unique in revealing itself? Is creativity an end per se? Are there different models of creativity?

Chapter 5
Two Models of Creativity: Technological Innovation and Social Quality

Introduction: Defining the Creative Sector

Creativity matters. It matters in art, science, culture and, not least, in the economy. In Italy, in 2004 the macrosector of the cultural and creative industries accounted for just over 9% of GDP and employed more than 2.5 million people. The figures for other countries are similar: 10% in Sweden (2000–2001), 12% in Denmark (2000–2001), 5.8% in the UK (2003), and 3.3% in the United States (2002) (UNCTAD 2008).

Although since the 1990s there have been many studies of the sector, there is still no shared consensus on what a cultural or creative industry is.

One of the more wider-ranging definitions is the one adopted here, which adds a variant to the interpretation of the cultural and creative industries based on the production of content, their intellectual protection and the new communication technologies. This variant highlights the cultural value of the design-based industries associated with a model in which quality, tradition and material culture have a strategic role. Thus two models will be discussed: *creativity for technological innovation* and *creativity for social quality*. The two models are not mutually exclusive. They co-exist (especially in Europe) and arise with intensity in defining creativity and the cultural industries in terms of national experience.

Creativity and Social Quality: The Emergence of a New Model

Ongoing Progress in the Cultural and Creative Industries

The last two decades have seen considerable growth in the importance of the cultural industries. This has been a result of the increase in global demand for their products, stimulated by *the New Economy* and by a new qualitative phase in

W. Santagata, *The Culture Factory*,
DOI 10.1007/978-3-642-13358-9_5, © Springer-Verlag Berlin Heidelberg 2010

the economy of material culture or the economy of goods for people and their living conditions

The reasons for the growth in demand in the cultural and creative industries may be briefly summarized as follows:

1. The development of *the New Economy*, driven by *ICTs* and *the Internet economy*, which have their origins in key scientific innovations (computer science, information and communication science, digitization, the Internet and software applications), has made it possible to produce instruments and equipment for the consumption of audiovisual culture which is now accessible to billions of people worldwide at relatively low costs. There has also been an enormous growth in the demand for culture, following increased schooling and urbanization, the emergence of meta-cities, and a rise in incomes and individual wealth. This worldwide trend has pushed up the demand for content-industry goods (publishing, films, music, audiovisual products, museums and libraries), and simultaneously for the goods of the cultural industries and auxiliary services supplying the cultural and creative markets (advertising, legal systems and education).
2. New trends have also emerged in the international trade system, both in terms of increased exchange and the variety of products traded. The concessions introduced by new trade treaties have made it possible to go beyond the old logic of trading natural resources and labor from emerging countries for high-tech goods or goods with symbolic value produced by advanced industrial countries. In particular, the huge market for material–culture goods, i.e. the market for all the goods and services produced for a person's survival, protection, leisure, entertainment, culture and well-being, has not only expanded and been consolidated but has also become fairer and more open. The market for goods based on material culture is radically changing, thus shifting from competition based on low production costs to competition based on the quality of products, their symbolic value and the quality of the experience which they offer. Consequently, the vast production sector of material–culture goods (industrial design, designer fashion, house design and household goods, lifestyle, tourism, the wine and food industries, and light engineering), is being driven by a rise in demand for quality products expressing aesthetics, decoration, design and traditional knowledge.

Culture and Creativity

Culture is our history, our present and the inheritance we leave to future generations. Culture is an inexhaustible source of wealth. The more culture is consumed, the more culture itself grows and encourages people to grow, understand identity and realize their potential.

Creativity can be found in culture, in the territory we live in, in the quality of our everyday life and the products we use. It is not an end in itself, but a process, an extraordinary means for producing new ideas. In this sense, creativity and culture are the pillars of social quality, seen as a context of a free, economically developed, fair and culturally lively community with a high quality of life. Creativity and culture are inextricably bound. They are a successful combination which in periods of strategic transition can position a country in the international process of globalization. The creative industries in Italy and France, for instance, look not only to advanced countries and their technologies, but also to developing countries and their great cultural traditions. With the former they share history and institutions, and with the latter the territorial presence and social bonds in which culture is (for the most part) tacitly transmitted. They compete with advanced countries, albeit with difficulty, in the knowledge economy and innovation, while with developing countries they collaborate in enhancing the value of the culture and creativity of those countries.

Why Producing Creativity and Culture Is a Key Objective for a Modern Society

As we have seen, if we classify cultural policies in functional terms, there are four general types, the first two with negative values and the other two with positive ones: on the one hand there are policies of cultural destruction and the neglect of cultural goods; and on the other are policies for the conservation and production of culture (unfortunately, many countries do equally in all four classes). What we must now concentrate on is reacquiring our capacity to produce new culture, a concept which has come to include all evidence of civilization and every expression of the historic and artistic heritage.

In Italy, for instance, we have conserved, managed and safeguarded the cultural heritage. We have also allocated a good deal of public and private resources to them. But the time has come to dedicate far more resources to the production of new culture. We must stop destroying our landscape. We must invest in education, training and research to promote technological progress. We have forgotten that things never stand still and that in the increasingly high performing world of creativity and the cultural industries only those who are ahead of the field will continue to be leaders.

The economic development of the cultural industries is strongly indebted to the phenomenon of creativity. Creativity is an asset in economic development for several reasons:

- As an input of aesthetic, decorative and design processes, creativity has an impact on the intangible component, which includes products' intellectual property.
- As an input of innovative technological processes, creativity has an impact on innovation, productivity and technical quality.
- By adding a symbolic dimension to products, creativity has an impact on demand and competitiveness.
- Creativity tends to lead to the reorganization of companies around an "epistemological community" (Creplet et al. 2003) and a "community of practice"

(Wenger 1998). We thus find a kind of joint presence of an intellectual/artistic/aesthetic/cognitive spirit and a more economic spirit (focused on the market and organizational rules).

Models of Cultural Production and Creativity

Culture and creativity combine in diverse ways according to the historical conditions in a given country, giving rise to partly different models. In some countries technological aspects prevail and technical innovations play a dominant role, while in others economic aspects related to the development of markets and business prevail. In some, legal aspects and the application and development of copyright prevail, while in others cultural aspects, based on tradition and social quality, are the dominant features. Although the differences between countries' models of creativity and cultural industries are expressed more in terms of shifts in emphasis than in content, we can nonetheless outline two distinct profiles. This is not a neutral exercise because each profile ultimately contributes to defining and identifying various sectors in the domain of the cultural industries.

Creativity for Innovation

The first profile considers creativity and the production of culture as input which comes from the knowledge society (according to the strategy of the Lisbon Agenda, approved by the European Union in 2000), communication technologies, scientific and technical innovations and the content industries. It is this vision that informs the British and Scandinavian approaches and the approach commissioned by the European Union (KEA European Affairs 2006). We will call this model "creativity for innovation." Creativity is defined in relation to innovation and to an industrial model of producing cultural content. The focus in this approach is on scientific research, markets, new business models, and marketing products and creative services. In a variation to this approach – elaborated by the World Intellectual Property Organization (WIPO) and widely used in the United States – the production of culture and creativity are enlisted to spur development in the production of intellectual property. The cultural and creative industries taken into consideration are a subclass of those on which assigning copyright is based: audiovisuals, films, music, software, the performing arts and publishing.

Creativity for Social Quality

The second profile conceives of creativity and cultural production as contributing input to social quality. We will describe this model as "creativity for social quality." It refers principally to the products of culture and social life and the sectors expressing them. There is a special focus on the world of material culture, a term from the field of anthropology that has been extended to sociological and economic analysis and embraces the enormous variety of markets of goods and services for people. Other important factors of progress in social quality include the growth of the content industries (film, radio and TV, publishing, software, and advertising) and the use and development of the cultural heritage (archives, libraries, museums, monuments, art, music and the performing arts). This approach enables us to identify a model of creativity and of the cultural industries, characterized not only by the logical coherence between the sectors included in the analysis (for example, it explains the inclusion of the food industry) but also its capacity to go beyond considering the impact of the culture industries only in terms of markets and business in order to highlight their great importance for social quality.

Further Details on Culture and Creativity for Social Quality

Social quality may be better defined as the extent to which people can participate in social, economic and cultural life and in the development of their communities in conditions which improve well-being and individual potential. At the same time social quality may be defined as everything that enables individuals to pursue variable combinations of actions both elementary (access to culture in its various forms and the cultural heritage, access to the fundamental goods of citizenship, enjoying good health and enhancing human capital) and complex (participation in community life and an increased capacity to realize one's goals) (Torino Internazionale 2005).

Culture is a major component of social quality, primarily because its production and consumption favors the development of the social fabric in terms of tighter community cohesion, better quality human relations, feelings of trust, willingness to co-operate, and a stronger sense of identity. All of this modifies the way we live, by making restraints less stringent and providing more, and better opportunities for enjoying life.

We could say, therefore, that the more creative writers and artists there are, the better the cultural and quality contents of life is; the more creative architects we have, the better our architecture and urban spaces. If there is a higher number of creative designers, we will be able to obtain better material cultural goods and with greater numbers of creative teachers, better education. More creative public policies in the field of social inclusion and cooperation will improve human relations; a more creative environment, and will allow more individuals to satisfy their plans of life.

Culture, Ethics, Art and History as Filters for Creativity

Creativity is an essential input in the production of culture. Yet creativity is not an end in itself. If it were, it would even be acceptable as in-built in activities expressing values which are not necessarily shared socially. For example, creativity generates great novels, but also hundreds of weekly hours of junk television; the Mafia and organized crime express forms of sociably deplorable organized creativity.

If creativity is not an end, as a means it must be interpreted and filtered by the culture of the community in question. Seen in this way, creativity is our way of pursuing socially shared objectives endowed with value, in both the cultural and technological fields. Italy with its qualities and faults is arguably a country in a good position to assess the production of new goods, creativity and innovation through the filter of its culture, ethics, art and history. As in the case of *naked technology*, originality or the abstract beauty of creativity are not enough. To become social quality, creativity must pass the test of culture and art. The advent of atomic energy was an incredible leap forward for human creativity, scientific research and innovation, but for it to become social quality it had to be shown that it could protect human life and guarantee a better quality of life. Ethical issues, which atomic energy per se does not address, needed to be faced through the refusal to accept destruction or a balance of terror.

Creativity, tempered by ethical, cultural and artistic values is thus an extraordinary means for producing new culture. Mass production and distribution of the new goods and services of the cultural industries and the continual search for and accumulation of material–culture goods and services enhance the quality of our lives. In many countries such as Italy, creativity and the culture industries can rely on spatial and temporal conditions for success, especially in the creative spaces of its cities and its industrial districts and local enterprise systems.

Culture as History and Local Territory

At the heart of the model of social quality, well illustrated by the Italian case, is the bond between our creativity and cultural production and history and the local territory. Time and space are the historical dimensions in which creativity emerges. The cultural industries and creativity are shaped by a local territory, which in Italy has primarily meant the production of material culture, the quality of urban space and the presence of industrial districts.

Culture is an idiosyncratic asset, specific to a spatially defined place yet able to communicate its content elsewhere in the world. Thus, for example, we have Hollywood for film culture, Murano in Venice for the art of glass making, Rome's ancient historical heritage, and Paris for fashion. Or, to cite an example in dance culture, we could mention the Calle Caminito, a small alley in the poor Boca quarter of Buenos Aires, where the tango originated and then went on to become an international cultural phenomenon.

The territorial origins of a culture and of the goods and services of its consequent cultural production do not follow standard patterns (Scott 2005) but after a chance beginning, grow and are expressed through a system of clustered economies. Our historic cities, many of our industrial districts, our performing arts and to a lesser extent our technological innovations have a long history of accumulating knowledge and experience.

Creative Cities and Creative Spaces

Creative cities and creative spaces represent in an exemplary and innovative way how space and time are at the origin and are the outcome of creative and cultural phenomena.

History is an accumulation of ideas, knowledge, mindsets, cultural atmospheres, identities and symbols. At each transition, successive generations enhanced creativity which for centuries has characterized the work and thought of the best talents. The context in which talents live influences the forms in which creativity and culture are expressed because the spatial phenomena of clustering are vital prerequisites for their production. The variables may include external economies, the production of trust and co-operation, pride, entrepreneurial energy, and the strengthening of a sense of identity (Scott 2000). In other words, the city has been and to some extent continues to be the ideal framework for the production and social distribution of creativity, intangible cultural goods and flows of information and knowledge. Today's cities are still meeting places of culture where dialogue provides vital new sap and energy.

A theoretical reconstruction of the value of local territory in explaining concentrations of creative talent has only been attempted relatively recently (Hall 1998, 2000). Hippolyte Taine was one of the first to speak of a "moral temperature" and the culture of the spirit which enables a talent to emerge at a given time and given place. The notion of a "creative milieu" was later taken up by others and is based on the free circulation of ideas, the accumulation of knowledge and the development in specific places of special expertise or skills (Tornqvist 1983).

Creative cities are also places in which culture and creativity show very high levels of social quality. This can be noted in lifestyles, the quality of consumption, cultural offerings, policies of social inclusion, easy access to the historic and artistic heritage, and the capacity to attract cultural tourism.

In Europe, creative cities are a phenomenon of great importance. They include not only large metropolises, but also small to medium-sized cities. Thousands of towns with ancient origins preserve the secrets of the strength of a local territory, its traditions, its capacity for social inclusion, and its communities.

In particular, the concept of space enclosed by walls, natural peripheries or defenses, once typical of the city, is a notion now being replaced by that of unbounded space defined by the local territorial area. Thus we no longer have cities of culture and culture is expressed in larger territories, which also give rise to creative and cultural experiences.

Cultural Districts or Clusters

Cultural district, or clusters, with their small industries or tourist attractions are another form of spatial experience rooted in the territory which, because of their cultural features, express a strong creative vocation. The vast majority of Italian industrial districts, which produce design goods based on the local culture and tradition, are also an example of cultural districts: from art ceramics in Faenza, Deruta and Caltagirone to stringed instruments in Cremona, textiles in Biella and Prato, and jewelry in Arezzo, Vicenza and Valenza Po.

In addition to the idiosyncratic nature of the cultural component of their products, these districts are characterized by a series of positive social and economic characteristics (see Chap. 7).

In these contexts, the most significant aspect of social quality pursued through the production of culture is cohesion and social inclusion, since the local social fabric encompasses cultural differences and develops relations of solidarity, favoring the individual and collective entrepreneurial spirits and the ability to pursue projects.

A particular new variant of the cultural district are *cultural commons* (Fiorentino et al. 2010). A *community cultural commons* is an economic resource giving raise to *social dilemma* defined by the confluence of three phenomena: culture, space, and community. As in the case of the Arte Povera artistic movement, the Mumbai film making community and other cultural commons, the social dilemma is identified with the uncertain transmission of the cultural commons to the next generation. The fading of new ideas nurturing the cultural community, can make the culture of the commons stationary. Cultural Commons basic characteristics include their public good nature and their endless carrying capacity.

Historical and spatial conditions alone are not sufficient requisites for a successful industrial culture. This also entails being able to guarantee a constant high level of creativity, and it is here that public policy is important. In particular, Italy should repeat the success of its historic cities and its material–culture districts in all sectors of the cultural and creative industries.

Conclusion

The need for urgent action may be seen as a wake-up call. We must attain the standards of the material and humanistic culture of our past without losing touch with technological culture, material culture and the content industries of the future. We should realize that the model of creativity for social quality marks the transition from policies designed merely to conserve culture (protection, restoration and management) to policies designed to produce culture. Such policies must provide solutions about how to select creative talents and how to increase the production of new ideas and transform them into new products to be marketed worldwide.

The two models – creativity for innovation and creativity for a social quality – are also an example of the North–South geographical divide which features on the international agenda. In fact, whereas the model of creativity for innovation and its insistence on technological aspects is typical of northern European countries, the United States and Canada, the model of creativity for social quality and its reference to culture, territory, society, cultural districts and creative cities seems to better interpret the trend in creative processes in Mediterranean, African, Latin

American and Asian countries. In this division of the world according to models of creativity, some countries, such as France and Italy, have an interesting bridging position between those who aspire to move the cutting edge of technological innovation towards ever greater success and those who want the progress of creativity to be constantly informed by ethics and the aesthetic and social quality of collective life.

Part II
Policies that Stimulate the Production of Culture and Make It Possible to Take the Lead in Strategic Sectors

Chapter 6
The Effects of Creativity on International Markets: The French Genius for Fashion

Is there anyone considered more of a creative genius than a stylist or haute-couture designer, untiring producer of ideas and good taste? The question may be a bit exaggerated, but it is obviously true that day after day, couturiers must engage in seeking creativity. Who more than their trusted manager was able to transform the old-fashioned factory or illustrious dressmaker's into a competitive international enterprise founded on the creation of ideas and innovative distribution methods?

The fashion world is naturally exposed to continual renewal in overall rate of creativity, which includes both the creativity involved in the product-design stage and the creativity connected to company management. We will therefore take the fashion industry and, more generally the fashion system, to serve as the basis of an analysis of the effects creativity has on markets and on international competition (Barrère and Santagata 2005).

There is yet another reason why it is useful to choose fashion as the object of our analysis. In fact, although genius and creation are phenomena linked to individuals, when they are viewed from a historical perspective, their collective dimension clearly emerges; in other words, we see their evolution from one generation to another. Thus one of the greatest challenges the fashion system faces is whether it will have the capacity to produce and renew a constant or growing level of creativity in each generation. This will lead us to examine the effects of a succession of generations of managers and designers in the light of the dynamics of international competition. The French fashion world with its exemplary history will be the basis of our analysis.

How Creativity Can be Renewed

The concept of a "field of forces" found in Pierre Bourdieu's sociological studies (1971, 1992, 1994) helps us understand the simultaneously conflictory and competitive nature of the fashion world. Like all fields of cultural production, the field of forces is a field of conflict. Bordieu described it as involving physical, economic

W. Santagata, *The Culture Factory*,
DOI 10.1007/978-3-642-13358-9_6, © Springer-Verlag Berlin Heidelberg 2010

and especially symbolic relations and being characterized by struggles to conserve or transform these force-based relations (Bourdieu 1998, 140).Within it is the entire fashion universe, constructed of symbols, objects, distribution systems, agents, economic organizations and institutions.

The fashion field comprises institutions, organizations and agents. No field exists without organizations: ateliers, haute-couture fashion houses, textile manufacturers and companies. No field exists without institutions: intellectual property rights, formal and informal conventions and rules. Institutions create incentives to act and structures that set limits; organizations exploit the opportunities which arise. Together they allow a field to emerge in which young stylists and creative managers struggle to acquire autonomy by differentiating themselves from other social roles. Finally, no field exists without agents who occupy a position in its structure: "namely in the distribution of symbolic capital whether or not it is institutionalized". That position "with the mediation of the dispositions constituting their *habitus* [...] leads them both to conserve and transform the structure of this distribution, therefore both to perpetuate the existing rules of the game and to subvert them" [ibid, 71]. The field is thus the space where the stylist's social function is constructed.

The contexts for coordinating the practices and the challenges of fashion design are thus the background to a complex network of enmities and friendships inherited from past struggles. They involve all generations – those that are emerging and seeking space by going against the couturiers at leading fashion houses, just as much as those that have been successful, dominate official production models and are in a position to control the processes which valorize collections.

For originality and innovation to emerge in a situation like this, it is essential that the field modify its structure and, as a consequence of the pressure exercised, that a new pole with new players be created. This can occur in a highly complex process of differentiation dominated by the lack of a single aesthetic principle that would make it possible to classify stylists in terms of a universal hierarchy of values. The factors consecration and legitimization are based on are not independent from market forces. The field's dynamics are continuous, implying perpetual revisions, rearrangements and redefinitions, produced anew with the arrival of each new generation.

The speed of change in the fashion field is marked by the succession of generations of creatives. The reasons for this originate in the definition of fashion as an idiosyncratic commodity, whose value emerges in space and time. The (often aleatory) conditions on which the success of the great couturiers was based occurred in a specific place (Paris), at a particular time (the 1950s). Time/space constitute a formidable force, one which defines a generation, creating an image that is both symbolic in its seductive capacity and concrete in terms of realization.

The evolution among Parisian couturiers is strikingly clear when we note the dates they entered the field. Significant phases of concentration can be discerned: after its origins in 1858 with Charles Frédéric Worth and Gustave Boberg, the turning point came in the twentieth century with Jacques Doucet, Jeanne Paquin, the Callot sisters, Jeanne Lanvin and Paul Poiret; then there were the years between the world wars marked by the arrival of Jean Patou, Madeleine Vionnet, Coco Chanel, Edward Molyneux, Lucien Lelong, Nina Ricci, Germaine Barton "Grès", Elsa Schiapparelli and Cristobal Balenciaga; and the post-war period dominated by creative geniuses such as Jacques Fath, Carmen Mallet "Carven", Pierre Balmain, Christian Dior, Hubert de Givenchy, Ted Lapidus, Louis Féraud and Pierre Cardin. Fashion in the 1960s bore the stamp of the inspired genius of Yves Saint-Laurent, Karl Lagerfeld, André Courrèges, Rosette Met "Torrent", Cacharel (Jean Bousquet), Jean Louis Scherrer, Emanuel Ungaro and Paco Rabane; the 1970s saw the emergence of J. Charles de Castelbajac, Issey Miyake, Kenzo, Thierry Mugler, Jean-Paul Gaultier and Christian Lacroix; Tom Ford, John Galliano, Alexandre McQueen and Martin Margiela are the leading names in the contemporary period.

It is difficult to reproduce creativity and hand it down from one generation to the next without quality being lost. Nature distributes gifts and talent in mysterious ways; there is no guarantee that these will be inherited. Berlin in the 1950s or post-1989 was no longer the Berlin of the Weimar Republic. Ideas age, customs change, styles evolve. The result is that each generation has an identity of its own, a distinctive personality.

Conscious of what can happen, public institutions and the fashion industry seek to make generational renewal as painless as possible in a given space–time context (minimizing costs and maximizing advantages).

Creativity and Generational Succession

Creativity is nourished by systemic effects and synergies between creators and institutions; in addition, creativity in objects and creativity in organization stimulate one another.

A creative environment fuels itself and history seems to indicate that once the critical mass needed for creativity has been reached, there is a surge that lasts the life of a generation. Certainly, the birth of new creative talent is basically in line with a time-discontinuous, stochastic process but circumstances or the social environment can generate unusual conditions that provide the necessary creative critical mass and produce concentrations of talent, situated in space and in time.

It was these factors that produced the famous spate of creativity in French fashion in the 1950s and 1960s, a wave on which Christian Dior, Hubert de Givenchy, Pierre Cardin, Pierre Balmain, Yves Saint-Laurent and Karl Lagerfeld rose to success. The wave had high visibility, all the more when we take into account the diffusion effect connected to the phenomenon of numerous imitators, copiers that never approached the great designers' excellence. Their products, whose quality ran the gamma from very low to mediocre, helped to focus attention on the crest of the wave. This phenomenon is typical of fashion and leads us to the strategic question of generational succession in creative fields.

Why was it only in the second half of the twentieth century that people began to show an interest in creativity? Concentrations of talent had existed before then, but the first thing we notice is that the majority of the fashion houses founded in the first half of the twentieth century did not survive their founders: Madame Vionnet, Poiret, Worms, the arbiters of elegance in a glorious era, had nearly all gone out of business for lack of an heir: a generation of people who were irreplaceable and were not replaced.

On the contrary, the fashion houses that came through the tragedy of the Second World War, were to have a better chance of surviving their founders. It is as though the value of the brand name and its symbolic content had become greater than the value of the individual couturier's creativity and thus no longer depended on it. In fact, the growth in the size of the market and number of customers, and especially the new production of luxury accessory products, which contributed to increasing the fashion houses' fame without directly involving the savoir-faire and creativity of their founders, made brand autonomization possible. A brand name could acquire an image of its own, detached from the personality of its original creator. Perfume and fashion accessories in particular were able to confer increased value on a brand. Chanel, for example, was one of the first firms to survive its creator. Reputation had thus become capital in which to continue to invest. From this time on, the generational waves of creativity, unpredictable and aleatory per se, did not vanish when a creator retired or died. Thus the problem of succession arose.

Add to this that fashion houses were no longer family-run businesses. Once ownership had passed to shareholders, succession became almost routine. The phenomenon can be better understood if we compare French and Italian haute-couture and *prêt-à-porter* firms. The former have a differentiated structure and are not family-run: a variety of players contribute to their financial success. Italian firms instead, were at least in part controlled by their founders' families, whether we are speaking of Armani, Prada or Missoni. This made succession in Italy more complicated, as it is easier to change shareholders than to replace one creative personality with another.

To all this must be added the existence of a cosmopolitan tradition in Paris, which had long demonstrated the ability to welcome talented individuals no matter what their name, nationality or social origin might be. The best-known designers do not seem to fear changing country or continent. They aim at no particular target group or brand. While in Italy companies and even consumers are heavily dependent on the founder, Paris fashion benefits from a cosmopolitan tradition that guarantees scandal- and regret-free intergenerational succession. Many of France's couturiers were foreigners, including those least known by the non-specialist public (Pierre di Alby, né Giorgio Vaskène in Armenia; Chloé, née Zyga Pianko in Poland; Egyptian-born Gaby Aghion), and those famous throughout the world (Charles Frédéric Worth, Cristobal Balenciaga, Elsa Schiapparelli, Nina Ricci, Pierre Cardin, Emanuel Ungaro, Karl Lagerfeld).

Thus the strengthening and autonomization of brands following their entry into the rich luxury accessories – leather goods and perfumes – and ready-to-wear markets, the transformations in capital structure and company control, the evolution from family-run firms into multi-national corporations, and finally the internationalization of talent made possible by the way designers from abroad were welcomed and integrated into the country's customs and traditions, contributed to modernizing generational succession and the transmission of creativity.

France's Creative Advantage

A creative wave is more than the invention of a style, new forms or an original aesthetic.

From the economic and organizational point of view, a new wave introduces fundamental innovations both at the process and the product level. Simply stated (see Fig. 6.1), it could be said that the great French wave of the 1950s and 1960s (F1 in Fig. 6.1) depended on the invention of the modern haute couture/*prêt-à-porter* twosome. Before this there was designer wear and there was off-the-peg apparel, but they existed as separate worlds, one elitist and innovative, the other monotonous, conformist and for a mass market. The French invention not only provided the industry with a seductive image and superior aesthetic quality, it also made industrial mass-production methods available to stylists.

The Italian wave of the 1970s and 1980s relied on the organizational flexibility provided by industrial districts and the creation of a production atmosphere in which micro and small companies formed a system, freely exchanging information and creating social capital. District-based economies fostered integration between design, technology, textile manufacture, artistic–artisan activity, and effective policies for expanding into international markets.

The subsequent success of U.S. fashion depended principally on mass distribution. Large department store chains conveyed to a mass public the creations of stylists interpreting the casual, informal taste typical of America's lifestyle. At the same time, the public's preferences were brought into line with stylistic and

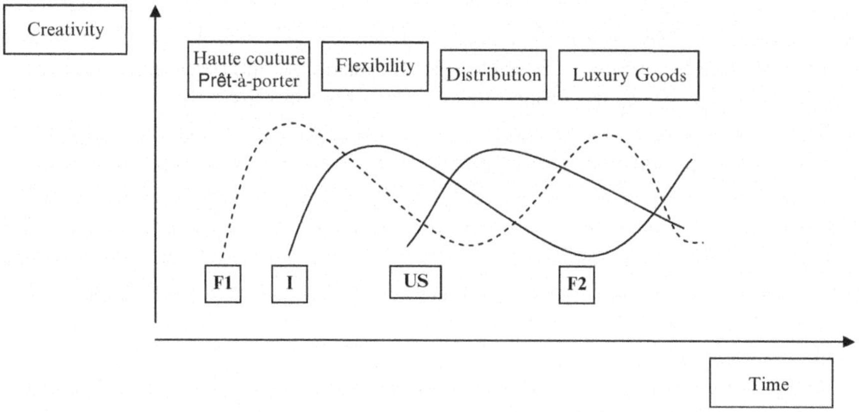

Fig. 6.1 The advantage of being the front runner

industrial decisions, making the distribution phase the most important one in the production chain.

The French creative wave, which revolutionized high fashion and facilitated the emergence of modern *prêt-à-porter*, was at low ebb from 1990 to 2000. A creative wave is in fact characterized by depreciation as time passes: when it first appears, the creativity quotient of the wave is at its height; afterwards, a slight loss can be perceived, leading slowly towards decline. This phenomenon seems to apply both to individuals and their creative impetus, as well as to overall systems, in which imitators who are masters of repetitiveness may depose brilliant pioneers. This trajectory occurred along parallel lines in France, Italy and the United States but in different time frames: the Italian wave took shape approximately 20 years after the French wave, the American wave 30 years after France's.

The Advantage of Being the First to Arrive

From the viewpoint of France's advantage in international economic competition, what counted was that the new French wave (F2 in Fig. 6.1) was gathering force at the same time as some Italian stylists (Moschino, Versace, Trussardi) passed away (naturally or tragically), others were beginning to look tired, and the country's creative wave was in decline. It had the same advantage over its American competitors. It can be said, therefore, that international competition in the world of fashion is influenced by a generational creative-wave factor.

This dynamic is illustrated in the history of French fashion. France was the first fashion-producing country that was forced to come to grips with the question of finding successors to its great designers: Dior, Balmain, Yves Saint-Laurent. In other words, in the 1950s and 1960s it was the first to see the emergence of a generation of creative stylists, and in the 1990s was again the first (F2) to face the challenge of bringing new talent into its great couturier companies: Tarlazzi at Guy Laroche; Ferré at Dior; Montana at Lanvin; Lagerfeld at Chanel; and then Galliano, Ford, Lacroix... We are therefore now seeing a new "French" wave, (with French in quotes because renewal is becoming increasingly international, looking to foreign talent to defend the reputations of its fashion houses).

The new wave relies on a creative innovation of its own: the launch of the mass luxury market. In addition, luxury *prêt-à-porter* has come to play an increasingly strategic role in this sector: not only is LVMH the leader in the luxury sector, it has also played a key role in selecting designers in the talent renewal process. Its honor roll is remarkable: Marc Jacobs (Louis Vuitton *prêt-à-porter*); John Galliano (Dior haute couture); Alexander McQueen (Givenchy); Heidi Slimane (Dior, men's fashion); Tom Ford (Yves Saint-Laurent); Christian Lacroix (who went on to found his own couture label).

The groups in the luxury industry have been the moving force in relaunching French fashion brands. Much of their new talent comes from abroad, something which causes no embarrassment since the question of nationality can be seen in two ways: either the creator's culture is not influential and so no problem exists or else it is important and the company decides to use this specific culture to penetrate new foreign markets. This may explain the success of talented individuals from the U.S. and U.K. Dior's choice of Galliano was risky, but was a calculated risk. As Bernard Arnault, one of the pioneers of new French luxury goods market, wrote, "Choosing a creator is always difficult. It's not a question of taking a talented creator and saying, 'We'll employ the person in such and such a business and it will work'. It isn't true. It's far more complicated. We need to find the talent, the ideas and the personality that can adapt to the spirit, the history of the brand" (Arnault 2000).

What applies to Galliano working at Dior also applies to Lagerfeld being hired by Chanel. Each creator finds utmost expressive ability in one particular fashion house.

The challenge, therefore, is multifaceted. For the French, it was a question of exploiting the advantage of being in the lead. The strategic option that enabled France to transform this theoretic advantage into an industrial one was the development of French superiority in the creative luxury goods industry. The luxury industry emerged as a double innovation – product and financial strategy – of the French creative wave at the start of the new millennium. Paraphrasing the title of the Arnault's autobiography [ibid], we could say that luxury is a French creative passion. But alongside this, prestigious and effective educational opportunities must be developed, since France seems to be falling behind, especially compared to U.K. and U.S. schools and on-the-job training in Italy's industrial districts, a trend we will focus on in the next chapter.

In fact these districts, in their cultural version, are a vital factor in the production of material culture. It is not easy for them to remain successful in the international arena and this means they continually need to acquire new ideas and organizational creativity: they must, in short, produce culture.

Chapter 7
Potential Cultural Districts and the Production of Material Culture

Creating cultural districts is an example of an economic policy that has been extremely successful in bringing together culture, managerial creativity and industrial design. These special industrial and artisan agglomerations will be the subject of this chapter, as they are an example of how culture and creativity can be the moving force in sustainable local economic development (OECD 2005).

Developing systems of micro and small enterprises or concentrating business activities whose products and aims are similar are phenomena that are generally well situated in time and space, as they depend on the birth and evolution of material culture and the production of goods and services that have delineated a territory's environmental and cultural habitat. The ancient writings of Mediterranean, Oriental and Asian civilizations, and the chronicles of medieval Europe, provide a wealth of examples of concentrations of micro-enterprises which in time evolved into potential or real industrial districts. In a few cases these agglomerations produced an external economic fabric that was sufficient for maintaining endogenous economic development (Murano, Caltagirone, Sheffield, Soningen and Grasse come to mind). In other cases, especially in developing countries, there are concentrations of this sort that demonstrate great potential but are still something less than a district; if they are to become cultural districts there will have to be institutional intervention– encompassed roughly between procedures for assigning intellectual property rights (Santagata 2002) and the stipulation of territorial agreements, (Magnatti et al. 2005) – that could redefine the individual and collective incentives of the economic agents in the given territory.

In theoretical terms a cultural district arises at the confluence of two phenomenon: the presence of external economies of agglomeration and the idiosyncratic nature of culture. When these two factors are brought together in a dynamic, creative economic environment, the basic conditions for the existence of a potential cultural district are satisfied. The addition of efficient institutions is the political factor that can permit a potential district to be transformed into a successful, real phenomenon (Santagata 2000, 2002, 2006).

It is now time to describe the fundamental points of the theory of cultural districts and show how these have been put into practice in a variety of ways

W. Santagata, *The Culture Factory*,
DOI 10.1007/978-3-642-13358-9_7,

which, taken together, describe the major fields of applicability of district-based economic policies. Some types of cultural district in fact correspond to industrial systems where small firms produce material culture's traditional goods (textiles, ceramics, jewelry, designer objects, etc.), while in others the emphasis is on offering services rather than goods (museum districts, production systems for the performing arts and folklore) and on a less cohesive form of agglomeration between the participating firms (historical heritage and cultural tourism networks, archaeological sites).

The Theoretical Basis of Cultural Districts Marshallian Localized Industries and the External Economics of Agglomeration

Alfred Marshall (1890, vol. IV, ch. X; 1919) was the first to draw attention to localized industry. He theorized that industrial districts have the following advantages: (a) the free spread of information and ideas ("... the mysteries of trade become no mysteries; but are as it were in the air"); (b) the rapid spread of technical, processing, and in general organizational innovations; (c) the development of subsidiary trades in surrounding areas; (d) reduction in cost per unit thanks to the introduction of specialized of machinery and the increased use of specialized equipment; (e) the creation of a stable market for skilled workers, given the district's high concentration of firms.

Marshall's penetrating insight lent itself to further development. Thanks to the relevance of external economies of agglomerations, average production costs of firms in a district decrease, just as internal economies of scale reduce costs in large factories. At the end of the nineteenth century, when Marshall was writing, economists were aware that developments in transportation and the widening of the labor market would make industrial districts increasingly less competitive. The era of big business was already taking shape on the horizon. From this viewpoint, for example, the shift to mass production was one of the factors that ushered in the decline of some of the world's renowned districts, such as Sheffield in the U.K. and Saint-Etienne in France.

However after nearly a century, as experience has shown in Italy and elsewhere in the world, Marshall's hunch has turned out to be a valuable one; in fact the Fordist production model has ceased to deliver results. The industrial districts in what is called "the third Italy", are an excellent example of sustainable endogenous economic development (Becattini 1987; Bagnasco 1988). As part of this renewed interest in the district approach, it has been seen that while the presence of small business is still a fundamental element, the presence of a large number of small business in an area does not per se constitute a district. One of the salient characteristics of a district is interdependence between the goods and services it produces: in this type of "industrial atmosphere", (Marshall 1919) frequent contacts favor the exchange of specialized input and continuous, recurrent transactions stimulate the circulation of information and technology. In synthesis, within a district it is easier to find contractors, verify the quality of goods and services, and sign standardized contracts; in addition, tacit knowledge, mutual trust and the accumulation of social capital are other pervasive traits of local society and culture.

Culture and the production of cultural commodities are idiosyncratic

The second essential component in the theory of cultural districts consists in the idiosyncratic, particular, localized nature of culture and the production of culture-based commodities. Despite the universal spirit of culture, the districts that produce commodities connected with a local culture tend in fact to be characterized by idiosyncratic constitutive elements (Santagata 2000; Scott 2000).

In ancient times, when societies were simple, the origin of artistic culture was linked, in terms of consumption, to demand and to the needs of four social classes, conventionally the aristocracy, knights, merchants and the clergy. Although the demand expressed by these groups formed the fabric on which a local culture was based, obviously its specific content also depended on the supply of tangible local resources (soil/mines, climate, water, mineral resources, accessibility) and intangible ones (court patronage, universities, monasteries, centers of learning) (Harris 1977). What I would like to suggest here is that the presence of natural and institutional resources combined with a demand for goods and services from the most dynamic social classes is the basis of an idiosyncratic culture.

Commodities based on culture are among the most particular and specific of the vast range of goods human beings produce. In fact culture has two deep-reaching anthropological roots: time and space. The production of culture is indissolubly linked to a place or, in a social sense, to a community and its history. This idiosyncratic feature means that culture is an atypical commodity in terms of the market economy, which is principally related to generic goods, outside time and without a spatial dimension (Salais and Storper 1995). In this sense, the market becomes an imperfect institution, for example when it has to regulate the production and consumption of culturally-based commodities, such as fashion, design and art objects. The more culturally specific a commodity is, the less the pricing system is able to furnish relevant information and the less competitive market logic can function as well as expected.

Add to this that the creative element in culturally-based commodities is per se a historically specific, original product of a given generation. In painting, industrial design, filmmaking, fashion, and even in decorative motifs for ceramics, we can observe waves of creativity that rise and fall through generations (Santagata 2004). Thus the time/space duo has incredible force in creating a generation's reputation. At the beginning of the twenty-first century, it makes no sense to produce ceramics identical to those made in the Fifties: there have been changes in ideas, culture, communications and sales techniques, styles. What follows is that each generation has an identity, a pace, a creative streak of its own; in short, its own culture.

Cultural districts are defined by the production of idiosyncratic commodities based on creativity and intellectual property. Filmmaking, the audio-visual sector, the vast field of industrial design and production of arts and crafts, museum services, and the wine and food industries, all draw inspiration from a cultural and intellectual link to a specific local community. This strong connection to a social context and its historic evolution is the basis of competitive advantage as it represents the accumulation of localized cultural capital (Throsby 2000). This can be either *tangible* capital [historic monuments, museums, archaeological sites], *intangible* capital (shared values, ideas, customs, beliefs), and *material culture* capital, the most ancient evidence of civilization.

A cultural district, finally, is characterized by strong district-based presence of personal knowledge and what Polanyi (1958) and Polanyi and Prosch (1975) called tacit knowledge. The concept involves an information system that is a local public good, which is non-excludable and is circumscribed within a communal space defined by the personal experience of each individual in it. Technological and cultural information circulates freely: it is transmitted via tacit systems of communication, since there is a gap between technology, art, culture and the essential facts of real experience. Cultural commodities are idiosyncratic not only because tacit knowledge is needed to create, produce and distribute them but also because this knowledge is based on people's prior idiosyncratic experience: personal and collective history count.

Models and Types of Cultural Districts

The idiosyncratic nature of culture associated with the development of external economies of agglomeration will therefore be the basis of the present interpretation of the birth of a cultural district. However, the form a cultural district assumes and what is in it can vary depending on its social and economic origins, the existing cultural heritage, the technology it employs, how intellectual property is protected, and what local policies are enacted (Santagata 2000, 2002, 2003a, 2003b, 2004, 2006, Sacco and Pedrini 2003; Cuccia and Santagata 2004; Jalil Moreno et al. 2005).

Potential and real cultural districts: the institutional cultural district as a solution

Many types of cultural districts are an effective reality, capable of using culture as a driving force to kick start economic development, job creation and the production of revenue. The *industrial cultural district*, the most widespread model, follows the formula that in the Sixties and Seventies led to the international success of many of the "Third Italy's" small and medium-sized firms. Industrial cultural districts are an example of endogenous growth based on the presence of small businesses and specific forms of social regulation at the local level.

The basic features of the evolution that lead to the establishment of districts of material culture are a local community which is cohesive in terms of cultural traditions and the accumulation of technical knowledge and *social capital*; a high birth rate of new companies, resulting from *social capability* and *interactive learning*; and in general, the ability to think in terms of systems and to generate positive externality in the fields of design, technological innovation, managerial organization, product creation, job–market flexibility and commercial distribution. In economic terms this means that inside cultural districts, the costs connected to *the use of the market* are lower than elsewhere, thanks to the intense creation of positive externality, tacit knowledge, a high rate of innovation, networking, and the nearly cost-free spread of information.

Famous examples of industrial cultural districts include Hollywood for filmmaking, Prato in Tuscany and Biella in Piedmont for textiles and clothing, Murano for art glass, and Grasse for perfumery; the manufacture of jewelry, musical instruments, designer objects and many other goods in districts in developed and developing countries.

Yet given their intrinsic qualities, it is not always possible to utilize the logic of the cultural district as a political means to develop a local economy. No *specific factor* exists that can create entrepreneurial spirit. A district has no explicit date of birth. There do exist, however, especially in developing countries, interesting potential contexts. There are agglomerations of micro-enterprises that produce goods and services based on culture, but are something less than a district and need to be supported by a system of individual and collective incentives. In other words, there are potential cultural districts, but there is a lack of good institutions and good *governance*.

A possible solution for transforming potential districts into real ones is to use collective intellectual property rights as the basis of promoting market incentives to support local development.

It is therefore important to look closely at what an *institutional cultural district is*. Its distinguishing characteristic is its being rooted both in the formal institutions that assign intellectual property rights and brand names in a restricted territorial area of production, and in the local public institutions that can assist productive activities with financial, marketing, communications and professional training services. The legal protection of products and the economic incentives linked to the use of collective brand names, make possible, as we will see in the next chapter, tighter control of the production and distribution processes, with a significant increase in product quality and profits. Local public assistance facilitates the development of entrepreneurial ability, a spirit of cooperation and access to markets at home and abroad. The content of the goods produced in these districts is closely connected to local civilization and culture. In this case culture has global relevance given that it can mobilize the district's aesthetic, technological, anthropological and historical content.

Remarkable Cases of Potential Institutional Cultural Districts

Industrial cultural districts of material culture

In many contexts the industrial cultural district can prove to be a potential phenomenon that with the intelligent application of institutional rules can be valorized and transformed into reality. This is particularly true when it is goods and services of material culture that are being produced (Jalil Moreno et al. 2005). Once again, the Italian experience is emblematic. The agro-industrial cultural districts in areas such as the Langhe in Piedmont and Chianti in Tuscany are examples of the success of policies of assigning collective property rights and the important motivating role played by workable local policies. There are many potential cultural districts in the world: from Sigchos in Ecuador, where artistic ceramics are produced, to Aleppo in Syria, where micro-enterprises produce soap using traditional, three-millennium old methods, to Lucknow in India's Uttar Pradesh, where artisans embroider *chikan* fabric. The list could go on (Santagata 2006) but before examining other significant examples of potential cultural districts, it may be useful to cite an experience from Italy's artistic ceramics sector.

The ceramics district of Caltagirone is an emblematic example. The city has been known since ancient times for its beautiful ceramics, the elegance of its traditional design and the creativity of its craftspeople. Earth, fire and creativity, the three essential ingredients in ceramic production have been furnished from time immemorial by the area's clay pits, its woods, and by the cultural spirits that surround the city.

This is a small cultural district. It has fewer than 150 ateliers and workshops, each of which corresponds in terms of size to an extended family.

What principally distinguishes it from vertically integrated technological districts, Hollywood's filmmaking industry for example, are the following three factors: the intensity of division of labor; the level of technological innovation; the varied range of its products.

In the Caltagirone cultural district, we find horizontal integration between firms, little division of labor, and technological innovation stagnating. In fact when a cultural commodity's structure is elementary – ceramic tableware or art glass, for example – the entire product line can be turned out by small workshops run by artisans whose skill and creativity are the fundamental input which distinguish one company from those selling similar products.

Consequently in this type of cultural district, many small-sized productive units have the same relative positive external influences and social practices developed within the district, but are in bitter competition with one another. In addition, each productive unit tends to fully integrate the creation, production and distribution phases in the value chain. In particular, each firm tends to have its own showroom and point of sale – in its city, abroad or as an Internet website. To consolidate its international reputation, increase product quality and draw maximum benefit from influences outside the district, people in Caltagirone are considering creating a collective brand name.

Districts and Museum-Based Cultural Systems

A second example concerns museum networks. Museum districts are situated in cities' historical centers. Their density in itself creates systemic effects that attract visitors and tourists. The museum cultural district in general is the outcome of public policies, whose success factors are the existence of a localized culture, incorporated in human capital and in museum collections, and institutional start-up, represented by the local authorities' decision to create a museum district. Careful urban planning, aimed at the economic valorization of the city's artistic and historic heritage by using innovative networking capable of producing a strong collective image (brand), determines how the district should be constructed. The challenge facing museum districts consists not only in bringing together individual cultural units, but also in creating a new, more ample and systematic unit that represents far more than the mere sum of the original parts. Interesting examples include the museum island (*Museeninsel*) in Berlin, the museum district (*Museums-Quartier*) in Vienna, with forty structures devoted to modern art and culture, or the system of the House of Savoy's Collections in Turin.

Tourist Cultural Districts

In many developed and developing countries, the type of district described above are being transformed into cultural-tourism districts. These are represented by concentrations comprising activities related to accommodation and hospitality (hotels, bed and breakfast establishments, restaurants, tour operators, transportation services), the offer of traditional cultural services (historic heritage, museums, folklore, traditional medicine, spas) and the production of craft goods and material culture.

The idea of developing a composite tourist product in terms of a system or cultural district is relatively new. The aim is to valorize all local activities, generating maximum synergy and contributing to establishing an image and international reputation as a tourist destination. It differs from both luxury "five-star" tourism and the "all-inclusive" tourism approach, which in general are closed models, supplying services exclusively for their own clientele. Cultural tourism, instead, by definition dialogues with the local system, its cultural heritage, artisan products, way of life and folklore. The focus is less on large hotel complexes than on the revitalization of local attractions for a public that is seeking not luxury but culture, quiet, a natural environment and what has been dubbed edutainment. Precisely because image is vital, policies for managing the local collective brand names have proved to be a strategic way of informing the clientele of a global market, and, above all, as will be seen in the next chapter, of improving the quality of the products and services on available. Seen from this perspective, the cultural-tourism district is distinguished from hurried, low-cost tourism and is a little closer to the adventure tourism of young backpackers eager to see something new.

Cultural-Heritage Systems

These potential districts include a wide variety of cases and take the form of a circuit or a network connecting individual sites or monuments. Their economic valorization is strengthened by the production of collective services and the offer of a common identity. Impressive examples are Egyptian tombs (the pyramids, the Saqqara necropolis), the Khmer temples in Cambodia and the ancient cities of Sri Lanka.

America's Urban Cultural Districts

Urban cultural districts are injecting new lymph into their local communities, using artistic and cultural services to attract people, fight economic industrial decline and create a new image for the cities where they are located. An urban cultural district is a spatial conglomerate of buildings devoted to the figurative arts – museums and organizations that produce culture and goods connected to it; correlated services and structures. The majority of the world's cultural districts are found in American cities and in Great Britain, where the idea of the cultural district has been studied in theory and applied in practice starting from the first experiment in Glasgow in the 1980s (Forst Kumpf 1998; Valentino 2003; Sacco and Pedrini 2003). The standard metropolitan cultural district is founded on two institutional prerequisites: the existence of an urban area in which the structure of property rights is not overly parcelled out and the creation of a body or trust responsible for developing the project, expediting planning procedures and supporting the management and marketing of cultural activities. The plan for a cultural city would usually include an initial range of artistic and cultural services (museums, libraries, theaters, art galleries, art studios and shops); a second range of activities based on cultural production (workshops on arts and crafts, film studios, musical recording studios, local television stations); a third range of activities that constitute the complement needed to attract visitors and tourists (restaurants, cafés, souvenir and gift shops).

Districts for Contemporary Art: The Case of Beijing and the Chinese Market

The *Dashanzi Art District* in Beijing, also called *Factory 798*, is an outstanding example of a cultural district specializing in the production of contemporary art. It is a territorial system with artists' studios, galleries of Chinese and international art, and small businesses for developing an art market that has literally skyrocketed in recent years, and whose success has created the conditions needed for the development of a strong Chinese market in contemporary art.

The *Dashanzi Art District* is a system of abandoned factories – *Factories 798/706/797/799*, leased to artists and art dealers. Designed in Bauhaus style by architects from the former East Germany, it occupies 230,000 square meters with streets, buildings, squares, boulevards, galleries and restaurants daily filled with visitors, collectors, artists, art curators and cultural intermediaries (see Chap. 8 for a more detailed analysis).

Cultural Districts' Role in Developed and in Developing Countries

As happens with all social phenomena, the definition of cultural district has in a sense remained incomplete, since this is evolving together the transformations society and its economic structures are undergoing. Obviously, different types of districts are complementary and compatible, and taken as a whole demonstrate the potential role new strategies could play in economic development.

The distinctive features of the two principal models of cultural district discussed here, real and potential, can be summarized in five points. Although the two models can be found throughout the world, it will be useful to introduce a simplification. Real cultural districts, most of which are industrial ones, will be considered as an economic structure that works principally in developed countries, e.g. Italy, France and the U.K. Institutional cultural districts, in their many guises, will be considered in perspective as an economic formula that is particularly suited to developing countries.

Spontaneous Versus Institutional Models of Development

Differences in models of development depend on the way the institutions and collective rules that govern these districts have been established. While real industrial cultural districts in the West have an evolutionary historical model à la Nozick, the other model, conventionally associated with developing countries, is founded on a political project that guarantees intellectual property rights and draws up public cultural policies for promoting regional economic development. Our first consideration therefore concerns a cultural district's start-up.

The business ethos that evolves with and contributes to a real industrial cultural district's development has no specific starting date. Institutional re-engineering is not possible. What can be done, principally in developing countries, is to influence some of the mechanisms of a district's government by modifying individual economic incentives. This is what happens in an institutional cultural district where local institutions are able to transform a long, spontaneous process into a completed, real phenomenon. Collective property rights, such as conferring DOC status on wines in Italy or creating collective brand names, can serve as a vehicle for defining a high standard of quality, generate income and increase a potential district's competitiveness.

The Two Functions of Collective Intellectual Property Rights

In principle, conferring collective intellectual property rights has a twofold function. On the one hand, these rights are a safeguard against illegal copying of an idea or an industrial product. The principal rights concerned in this function are copyright, branding, industrial design, attestation of controlled origin and patents. On the other hand, rules, standards and mechanisms are introduced and promote the economic development of a geographic area, community or producers' association. While the first function is more relevant in developed countries, where the biggest problem is ensuring that real industrial cultural districts' products are not copied, the second is strategic for the economic start-up of micro and small businesses in developing countries, where the potential for local agglomerations must become real. When what is concerned are cultural-heritage systems and networks, the institutions involved are normally local policies.

Same Players, Different Structures

The two types of cultural district involve the same economic players: artisans, artists and entrepreneurs who produce culture-based goods. Localized micro and small firms run by artisans and small entrepreneurs exist everywhere, but because a higher rate of technology is employed there, vertical and horizontal integration of these companies is the pattern found in developed countries, while the agglomeration of a large number of identical, horizontally integrated micro-companies is the norm in developing ones. In both cases, given the essential features we have described, the ability to produce cultural goods and services is influenced by the positive outside influences that derive from localization. Where the cultural heritage is organized in networks, the chain of production is more likely to take the form of an integrated *filiera* with a wealth of museum, tourist and hospitality services, performances of traditional popular culture, and craft production. (Santagata 2003a, b).

The Material Culture's Goods and Services

The material culture's goods (functional objects) are supplied by both real cultural districts and by potential, institutional ones. While in developed countries the search for quality and design may be exaggerated, in developing countries product quality is guaranteed by tradition, unless it is the desire to lower production costs that prevails. The list of such merchandise is noteworthy (Jalil Moreno et al. 2005): natural food and beverages (wine, olive oil, fermented beverages, cheese); natural products and spices; textiles, clothing and fashion accessories (leather goods, glassware, eyeglasses, hats, gloves, umbrellas, watches); personal ornaments (jewelry, perfume); personal services (medicine and hygiene, hotels and restaurants, gourmet products, spas); decorative items (ceramics, terracotta, embroidery, glass, crystal, industrial design, plastic, porcelain); travel and transport; furniture;

entertainment and the cultural industries (serigraphy, musical instruments, newspapers and magazines, toys); publishing, arms and metallurgy.

Evolution

The economic development which has taken place in cultural districts has been positive in many ways. It has generated income, improved institutional capacity, increased openness to other cultures and made it possible to transmit creative ability to the young. There can however be disadvantages.

The decision to share the enjoyment of collective property rights depends both on individual incentives and on collective behaviour (Cuccia and Santagata 2004). If it is possible to join, it is also possible to withdraw. This means that while intellectual property rights are conferred permanently, individual participation can be temporary, given that withdrawal is an option. The principal function of a collective property right is to signal the average quality of a collective brand or logo, which means that those whose products are better than average will tend to pull out while those whose quality is very low will be excluded. In other words, there is a dynamic in the functioning of these rights that has a minimum threshold: below a certain threshold of quality, being identified with a collective trademark/the conferment of collective intellectual property rights has no advantages (even for free riders) and therefore is not chosen. The exit option seems to be a phenomenon that is present principally in developed countries, while in developing ones the scenario associated with low quality can be a dissuasive factor in conferring these rights.

In developing countries other possible disadvantages may paradoxically be linked to historic–cultural heritage systems being successful. In the first place, these countries often lack adequate public regulations on the use of land and landscape. Excess demand therefore generates costs in terms of congestion, which leads to the deterioration of tourist attractions: too many visitors, too many extraneous installations and ill-considered decisions – from hotel construction to privatization of public property. Secondly, external forces, such as powerful multinationals, can destroy the local culture by establishing new productive localizations that engage in unfair competition and exploit the local reputation. Globalization can endanger indigenous cultures and has already led to the destruction of some. These cultural invasions can be limited only by developing political instruments that protect the local culture and its economic activities. Of these instruments, intellectual property rights are now the most strategic.

Chapter 8
Intellectual Property Rights Take Command

Producing culture requires the use of special economic policy instruments, particularly strategies that boost a system's creativity, and the introduction of collective property rights, as it is this that can turn a potential cultural district into an operative one. This chapter will develop this last point, showing the reasons why intellectual property rights have become increasingly important in the knowledge society.

The Growth of the Intellectual Component in Goods and Services

Economists call the phenomenon dematerialization, by which they mean a process currently underway in which an object's material components count less in determining its value. Let us consider a wristwatch. Fifty years ago a watch might be made of gold or steel; its movement, with the springs, escapement and wheels that made it function, incorporated small rubies and the number of jewels in the watch was indicated on its face. Gold, steel and rubies together with traditional workmanship were the object's material content and, along with labor costs, accounted for a high percentage of the product's basic cost. The intellectual component in its manufacture (form, decoration, the watchmaker's technical know-how) counted little in determining its price.

Let us now consider a watch that symbolizes the revolution that has taken place: the Swatch. Its material component consists essentially of different types of plastic and a quartz mechanism whose basic cost is negligible compared to selling price. Its intellectual, technological, aesthetic and symbolic component is the dominant value. The product has been dematerialized and even watches that reproduce the forms and mechanical components of old-fashioned timepieces are now charged with strong intangible or immaterial symbolic value.

One of the consequences of the increase in the intellectual, intangible and immaterial component of a good is that the field of application of exclusivity associated with possession is modified. In fact, if I can exclude from consumption everything that is material simply by protecting it, caring for it and using it, the

DOI 10.1007/978-3-642-13358-9_8,

same cannot be done for intellectual goods. The form and the watch has and how it is decorated, the innovation of using a quartz mechanism, in short everything that can be reduced to an idea is a non-excludable public good, in fact something that can be copied and appropriated. An idea cannot be protected "physically", because once it has been revealed it can be copied and used without its originator's authorization. And as we are increasingly immerged in a universe of applied ideas incorporated into the material things that are part of our everyday habitat, we are increasingly becoming prey to intellectual piracy and counterfeiting (Benghozi and Santagata 2001).

Since someone with an original idea should be able to use it, reproduce it and derive income from it, whether it is a novel, song, painting, scientific invention or medical discovery, institutional means are needed to protect ideas. The most widespread method used is the creation of an ad hoc legal body which society recognizes and defends. It is normally intellectual property rights that are involved. However, providing legal protection is costly and these laws are not easy to apply. Other methods, industrial secrecy for example, are hardly applicable to cultural products whose very nature consists in external communication and the revelation of their contents.

Intellectual property rights are therefore gaining ground as the principal means of protecting ideas: they have taken command and dominate contemporary markets because they have become increasingly important in the production, distribution and consumption of goods, culture and technological know-how.

The principal forms of intellectual property have different forms of legal protection: patents for industrial inventions and technological innovations; copyright for creative work expressed in words, sounds and images; registered trademarks and distinguishing symbols for merchandise; design patents for industrial design; artists' resale rights for paintings and contemporary works of art. Clearly, culture, in the variety of forms in which it is expressed, can be amply protected by legal safeguards.

Copyright and Industrial Property Rights

Intellectual property rights can be divided into two broad categories: what in civil law are called author's rights, and copyright in common law; and industrial property rights.

Copyright concerns literature, including novels, stories and poetry; films and architectural design. One form of copyright, artists' resale rights, applies to the visual arts.

Industrial property includes inventions, protected by patent rights; individual and collective trademarks; industrial design and various ways of indicating guaranteed geographic origin.

Legal institutions therefore deal in depth with culturally-based goods, all of which are intangible and immaterial in terms of intellectual component, and protection has also been extended to related sectors. In fact those who interpret works of music or prose and producers of recorded music or television programs are also protected by what are called neighboring rights. It would be difficult to think of any good or service produced and exchanged on contemporary markets that did not receive some form of real or potential legal protection, either as a patent or registered trademark or else as copyright. It is this that allows us to say that such rights have taken command in directing and strengthening contemporary production systems.

Despite their importance, the arguments in favor of intellectual property rights are not completely convincing. In particular, although in some cases (for example patents) it is possible to define how long they should be extended and the optimal length of time that rights can be retained, in general it is not clear whether or not introducing intellectual property rights for cultural products is socially advantageous.

The dilemma is usually set out in these terms: on the one hand, copyright provides economic incentives for creators, while on the other it increases costs for consumers. These views could be further qualified, but in their elementariness they stand up, although in some instances and markets, authors or inventors surrender their rights in exchange for a lump-sum payment. As was mentioned, markets select artists through the payment of copyright and royalties and artists can live relatively comfortably and be free to create without employers, publishers or patrons conditioning their work. However if the payment of royalties increases prices, overall consumption will fall, and since it is a cultural good that is involved, this may not necessarily be positive. In short, the dilemma is whether to opt for the frying pan of a monopolistic privilege that favors the creator, or the fire of curtailing cultural consumption.

I do not know what the way out of this dilemma is, but a solution may be implicit in the very nature of property rights. In principle intellectual property rights do not last forever, nor have they always existed. They were brought into being when the economic and social structure evolved to the point where immaterial goods had emerged, technology had made the consumption of images and sounds ubiquitous and there was a government apparatus that could guarantee that the law would be enforced. In the future it is also likely that intellectual property rights will evolve in harmony with socio-economic and institutional change. Some will disappear; others will become weaker; new laws will safeguard new interests. If the dilemma shows that the costs of making culture more widely available are too high and have become a hurdle to progress, an evolutionary approach seems to indicate that there will be a counterthrust so that they are reduced (starting, for example from making it more difficult to transmit them to heirs so that children will no longer be able to profit from the ideas of a parent).

Does this mean we should sit tight and wait for the social system to regulate itself? I don't think so. I think a criteria does exist and would like to put forward a proposal.

After all, intellectual property rights constitute a way to accumulate economic resources in various fields of art and material culture. Their effect is extremely helpful when a company (whether or not it is individually owned) that produces culture is starting out. Put plainly, the monopolistic privilege connected to awarding property rights can be justified in the start-up phase of a culture-producing activity, when markets are tight and difficult to break into. But when, for various reasons, the firm has become self-supporting and is in the black, there are reasons why it should no longer enjoy this right in full.

There is perhaps no good reason why the monopolistic privilege of DOC status conferred on Barolo and champagne should last forever. Commercial success can be used as a measure for deciding when such privileges should be withdrawn.

If we are in the presence of a dynamic process, it should be encouraged, eliminating areas of resistance and friction. This is a process, moreover, that should be evaluated differently depending on whether it is taking place in a developed or developing country. In developed countries the protection of intellectual property rights has unfortunately become the basis for actions of cultural colonialism, unequivocal cultural invasions and the destruction of "different" local cultures, as happened to filmmaking and music in many countries or to national languages, whose progressive disappearance has impoverished world culture.

In conclusion, we should consider a possible way to regulate intellectual property rights, amended to take into account both whether the cultural activities being protected are self-supporting and enjoy commercial success, and the degree of international domination of markets and cultural diversity that exist.

In a certain sense this tendency is already spontaneously taking place for some rights, as we will see in greater detail in the next section. For example, in the case of indication of geographic origin, we have witnessed the phenomenon of producers pulling out from collective rights and repositioning themselves on markets in terms of their individual brand names. An indication of origin such as "DOCG Barolo", attests to the quality of the winemakers allowed to use it. What may happen, then, is that the roads to success benefit certain producers who, once they realize they have developed a level of quality that is decidedly far superior to the level indicted by the collective brand name, decide to drop out and count on their own reputation and individual brand name.

This is a further example of how there has been evolution in intellectual property rights and how this has been closely connected to changes in market conditions. The rights are not perpetual and immutable in terms of social and individual utility. The example also shows that in specific conditions a return to individual brand names can represent a possible solution to the dilemma I have tried to clarify.

Individual Rights and Collective Rights

The distinction between industrial intellectual property and copyright is further intertwined with the difference between individual rights and collective ones.

The first of these that should be mentioned, given the controversy they have aroused, are artists' resale rights, which apply in the world of the visual arts. In effect, painters, unlike people who compose or perform music or writers and designers, do not enjoy copyright. A painting is sold at a given price as a real good, like an apartment, and there is no provision for the artist's partaking in any future increase in the work's value. It is for this reason that artists' resale rights, enforced in France since the 1920s, were the subject of an EU directive that extended them to all member states, starting in 2006. The artist's inalienable right to a percentage of each subsequent sale of an original work, starting from a given price limit, was recognized. The rule did not apply to the first sale, nor to ownership passing between private parties. Unfortunately it is difficult to enforce the directive. Artists are uninformed and unaware of their rights; intermediaries (dealers, auction houses) fear price rises and consumers prefer to purchase art in countries which do not recognize artists' resale rights, for example the United States (except for California).

Other collective rights were explained in the discussion of cultural districts and the production of material culture. They have many different forms, including certifications guaranteeing quality awarded by presumably independent third parties. Two versions are important in the present analysis: collective trademarks and indications of geographic origin. Both of these are open-ended: once you get it, you keep it. The difference between them can be traced principally to technical aspects of production and how each is linked with territory.

A collective trademark safeguards the producers associated with and identified by a chosen symbol, who share identity, know-how and a location. The trademark does not protect a local product, particular technology, or fixed unearned income. It protects reputation. In competitive situations it protects a brand whose reputation has been constructed by the members of the organization or association it belongs to. For example, the brand name "Monferrato" is a competitor of the brands "Venice" and "Sicily".

On the contrary the right to indicate geographic origin bars a certain product's entry into a certain market, even when it has become a common heritage. The know-how that goes into making champagne or Parmigiano Reggiano is protected and no competition is allowed. We cannot find "Parmigiano Reggiano" and "Parmigiano from Barcelona" on the market, nor will we see "Champagne" and "Champagne from Chile". In this sense, in the long term being allowed to label a commodity with a geographic indication is a privilege, to the point that many countries (including the United States) are reluctant, if not opposed, to signing international agreements that would bring the practice into general use.

As an instrument of economic policy for developing enterprises that produce culture, collective trademarks or certification of quality seem to be more welcomed by the international community. Like cultural districts, they have two parallel functions: on the one hand, they safeguard intellectual property, while on the other they are the basis of a procedure that facilitates improving the quality of a product or service.

Since this is particularly important for start-up in weak economies in developing countries, the final section of this chapter will examine how a collective trademark for a local product can be administered. The concept of collective trademark is used rather loosely in this text, realizing that its different forms (collective trademark, hallmark and guarantee of quality, certification of quality, indication of geographic origin) involve characteristics, effects and levels of international protection that vary widely.

The procedure that will be described constitutes a first series of actions, which careful legal examination will have to translate into precise legal measures.

A Procedure for Improving Quality Using Collective Trademarks

To understand what is meant, imagine you work in a potential cultural tourism district. You want to activate a policy of development based on the positive effects presumed to ensue from the conferral of a collective trademark. A cultural tourism district is a productive system whose success is founded on the valorization and sale of a composite product, consisting of services and goods connected to the local culture, as expressed in its historic heritage, material culture, gastronomic traditions, natural and environmental beauty.

Awarding a collective trademark to a community of economic operators is a practice that can be examined as a series of the different phases that are part of a single procedure. Each phase fills a specific function, but taken as a whole they aim to increase the product quality of the tourist destination and improve its image. What follows is no more than an exercise directed at showing the flexibility and richness inherent in the procedure.

First Phase: Founding the Organization That Is to Hold Title to the Collective Trademark

In principle the collective trademark, which represents the identity of the cultural tourism district, is of interest to all the local economic agents involved in supplying the tourist product. A district's collective trademark should therefore be the property of an association, non-profit group or a cooperative. In the case of a highly fragmented cultural district, with numerous economic operators working in it, an association seems to be the best choice, because the collective trademark is effectively the expression of a heterogeneous group of subjects working in the public, private and non-profit sectors.

All accredited members have the right to use the collective trademark in accordance with the rules established. The members may be private firms, foundations, non-profit organizations, local public bodies. They must all agree to being subject to periodic controls that monitor the quality of their products and services.

Second Phase: Setting Up a Coordinating Committee

This is a crucial point because the logic of collective trademarks means there has to be a coordinating committee responsible for controlling access to the trademark and defining the minimum level of quality required of members. The members of the proprietary association or organization must appoint a coordinating committee which should have power of jurisdiction over all the activities taking place in the district's territory. If the territory coincides with that of a municipality, the local authorities will be closely involved in administering the collective trademark.

The committee's principal tasks will be to select a logo to submit to the association for approval and to decide how to allocate the trademark to local consignees.

The committee can be seen as an self-regulating body, composed of representatives of the cultural tourism district: local authorities, companies in the tourist, hotel and catering industries, authorities in charge of monitoring the cultural heritage, artisan firms, artists and craftspeople, organizers of trade fairs, festivals and performances. Every activity involved in producing the tourist product must be represented because in principal every firm in the district has the right to use the collective trademark. In practice, use will depend on the relative level of quality and the firm's successful completion of the accrediting procedure.

Third Phase: Identifying an Image

The most delicate part of the process is doing the research on what image will best symbolize the district as a tourist destination. The image needs to be both clearly defined and appealing. It must communicate information about the site and give a convincing response to the tourist in search of a personal motivation for visiting it.

The image will be stylized and reduced to a collective trademark, which can be simultaneously articulated as a logo, drawing, song, label or slogan.

This work should be handed over to a specialized company (ideally an internationally recognized advertising and design agency), which will provide the specific versions to be used in various situations: advertisements in newspapers, on web pages, on the radio; labels for products and services; communication and information services.

Fourth Phase: Establishing What Minimum Level of Quality to Accept

Once installed, the coordinating committee will have to decide what standards are important to maintain and what tests firms need to pass in order to be granted authorization to use the collective trademark. The standards should be applicable to all the goods and services the cultural district supplies.

The committee will also have to establish procedures that determine how faithfully the criteria adopted are being respected by the firms that wish to use the logo. If a local firm comes up to the standard required, it will be authorized to use the collective trademark. If it does not, it will not be excluded from the association, but will be placed on a waiting list until it fulfils the requirements.

The core problem the committee will have to face is therefore defining a minimum level of quality for each good and service the cultural district offers. How should these standards be chosen?

On the one hand levels of quality are defined within specific categories of goods and services. For example, the list of the main features associated with hotel service includes numerous indicators of quality that define standards of personal safety, room size, reception and breakfast services, etc. The objective, therefore, is to select a level that is consistent with a good, yet realistic image of the hotel services available. Too high a level would exclude too many hotels from using the trademark; an overly low standard would discourage potential tourists.

On the other hand, quality concerns the tourist district as a whole, i.e. its tourist product. In this case the coordinating committee has greater freedom in its choices because what counts is the district's "average" and if a few sectors are not ready, the committee can ask them to meet the norms that have been established and wait for them to do so.

Fifth Phase: Registering the Collective Trademark

The fifth step is a practical matter: to be protected, the collective trademark must be registered with the offices which oversee intellectual property rights. The distinguishing mark chosen must conform to a few elementary rules that the office will check carefully before accepting it. In most countries anyone applying to register a collective trademark must furnish a copy of the regulations that govern its use, indicating who is authorized to use the trademark, the requirements for becoming part of the proprietary organization or association and the sanctions envisioned to prevent misuse.

Sixth Phase: Arriving at Decisions Through Compromise and Consensus

The members of the coordinating committee represent all the economic and political forces active in their cultural tourism district. As in any social and economic body, conflicts and negative confrontation may arise and consequently the decision-making process must be protected against unilateral decisions. This is why compromise and consensus should be preferred to majority rule. Before any decision is made, there should be discussion and analysis that clarify the costs and benefits involved, allowing each category to understand what is at stake. If governing through compromise prevails over majority rule, no-one will be excluded by a contrary decision, because to reach a compromise all parties must relinquish some demands and the decision taken is based on unanimous agreement (consensus). No minority will oppose a collective decision. Seeking consensus through compromise, safeguarding the rights of the weaker parties in the decisional process, is the best way to arrive at cooperative behavior.

Naturally, as each agent has the power of veto, reaching consensus on all questions could become inefficient. Consequently it is essential that the committee include authoritative members who can exert moral suasion.

Seventh Phase: Registration and Accreditation Rather Than Exclusion

When local public authorities are involved in the association/organization and become leaders in setting standards for admission to the collective trademark, checking periodically that members are respecting these standards may cause relational problems.

The association has the right to say no to firms whose products or services fall below the standards set. Candidates whose quality is substandard, cannot enter the trademark club and this could generate conflict and uncooperative behavior.

The political costs of being a cultural tourism district's guardians of quality could be unacceptably high for some institutions, which means that a more flexible, more constructive formula is needed. Actually there is a gentler way to turn someone down, involving a twofold procedure. The first step, registering the candidate, is completely open: everyone is accepted. All that is required is active participation in the district's tourist activities.

After registration the next step in the procedure is an initial evaluation of the level of quality of the new entrant's goods or services. If standards are met, accreditation follows, and as a regular member of the association, the candidate is authorized to use its registered collective trademark. If the quality level falls below the minimum set, an interactive process is set in motion, directed at guiding the candidate towards the minimum required. In this way, accreditation is the outcome of cooperative behavior that allows the district to achieve good average standards.

Eighth Phase: Evolution and Royalties

Administering the collective trademark can become sustainable in economic terms when royalties are obtained from sales to members of tags or labels to affix to the objects or presentations of services they supply.

If the role of the collective trademark is appreciated and backed by the local community, we can expect that both producers and consumers will be willing to pay for it (Cuccia et al. 2008). For example, a recent study on the economic valuation of a collective trademark for the shepherds in the city of Naples' nativity scene, showed that consumers' willingness to pay for certification of quality ensured by the collective trademark would make it possible to obtain the funds needed to cover the trademark's administrative expenses, including an advertising campaign in Italy and abroad, for promoting the city's San Gregorio Armeno cultural district.

Thus the complete procedure entails a minimum of eight phases which delineate a complex series of actions whose application principally concerns goods-producing sectors in the world of material culture and systems offering services connected to the valorization of local traditions and culture.

Chapter 9
The Cultural and Creative Industries

Two developments in the twentieth century profoundly influenced the cultural industry: the new expressive opportunities liberated by innovations in communications technology, and the enormous increase in demand for entertainment, design and works of art. Technological innovations made art ubiquitous in time and space, while industrial design made good quality modern furnishings available at accessible prices, and new forms of entertainment such as mass concerts, festivals and decentralized culture attracted audiences of hundreds of thousands of young people.

The inrush of new technology created sectors in which culture is produced with revolutionary means of expression. The list is short, but significant in terms of social and economic relevance: cinema, videogames, television, design, publishing, photography. From the time they first appeared, the success of these new artistic expressions was immense, showing how fully they responded to the needs and deep-rooted emotional drives in contemporary society. There were also disquieting, negative signs, whose importance may at times have been overestimated (Adorno and Horkeimer 1947), and at other times justly feared as cultural invasions of weak markets.

The new art worlds lost their unique aura and became subject to the rules of technical reproducibility (Benjamin 1936). New art commodities are mass-produced and exchanged on international markets which tend to be monopolistic and sensitive to the seduction of symbolic values, which makes it easy to sway consumers' choices.

What distinguishes the cultural industries as a category is their application of creativity to industrial mass-production and the pervasive intellectual component that characterizes their products and production processes. Their goods generally cost a great deal to produce and very little to reproduce or copy; they are high-risk products, which leads to monopoly-style alliances (Caves 2000).

The model of creativity and cultural industries which we have described in Chap. 5. has an equivalent in quantitative terms in a vitally important macro-sector of the economy. On the basis of the approach used so far, we can identify three spheres in which creativity is involved in economic processes characterized by the production of culture.

W. Santagata, *The Culture Factory*,
DOI 10.1007/978-3-642-13358-9_9,

Firstly, creative processes strongly influence the sphere of *material culture*. In this case creativity is mainly the outcome of a collective, local and cumulative process, in which the cultural element is an inextricable part of craft and everyday goods. Secondly, creativity is an input in the production and communication of *content* in the cultural industries which supply goods and services with a high symbolic content. This is the sphere of the content industries. Thirdly, creativity is associated with a country's *historic and artistic heritage*, made up of both its cultural capital (the outcome of the creativity of past generations) and contemporary artistic production.

These sectors have already been discussed in relation to cultural districts and will be further analyzed in this chapter. Here attention will be focused on the creative industries, whose industrial dimension conceals a problem of definition. In some cases, such as filmmaking, the product's creative component is evident: creativity and art are required to make a film; the fact that numerous identical copies are then produced is merely an extension of technological potential. Essentially, in filmmaking, TV, videogames, photography, industrial design and videography, technical reproducibility is based on an initial creative act which remains dominant no matter how much it is conditioned and assisted by new means of expression. In other cases, instead, judgment on whether culture is being produced needs to be suspended. It is difficult to tell, for example, whether Internet technology is merely an extension of the technological possibilities that preceded it, or represents an original factor in cultural production. In yet other instances, such as the record industry and publishing, the industrial dimension appropriates the original work and multiplies it so it can be sold. The impact on the production of culture is not direct (not the result of using new means of expression) but rather indirect (the result of mass-producing copies and distributing them).

Looked at more carefully, however, the distribution industries also play an important role in producing culture. Since the market is a powerful means of selecting artists, those who control the market indirectly control, at least in the short term, the production of culture, promoting artists and performers whose work is most in line with public taste. For example if a large recording company (note that the five majors – Sony, Universal, BMG, EMI, Warner – control over 80% of the world market) invests heavily in a musical genre, its penetration of international markets could be strong enough, at least in the short term, to favor that firm's musicians and, more importantly, to eliminate the products of any country incapable of competing in terms of production and promotion costs and the ability to set trends. Market control can give one cultural product an advantage over another, better qualified one, but an industry of this sort, whose principal functions are reproduction and distribution, should not be confused with one which directly produces new art commodities.

In this chapter it will not be possible to provide an exhaustive discussion of such a vast field of cultural production (Brosio and Santagata 1991; Bodo and Spada 2004; Benhamou 2000; Paris 2004; Benghozi 2006; KEA European Affairs 2006; The Work Foundation DCMS 2007; DEPS 2006; UNCTAD 2008; Santagata 2009). Instead, Italy will be used an example for those developing countries in which creativity is a potential, latent creative input, but the creative industries are having difficulty in taking off. As was seen in Chap. 7, in many countries in the world, there are cultural districts (agglomerations of micro-firms) in which we find companies involved in producing material culture. Often, however, the phenomenon gets no further than the planning stage. Even in other cultural sectors, from cinema to TV, from fashion to music, the real problem is how to spur local industrial start-up. Based on the situation in Italy, I will illustrate what constitute strengths and weaknesses in the entertainment and creative industries.

The Italian Cultural Industry at the Start of the Twenty-First Century

Using the classification implicit in the approach outlined in Chap. 4, we can identify 12 economic sectors characterized by creativity and the production of culture (Santagata 2009).

Table 9.1 shows the estimated economic value of the cultural and creative industries in Italy. If we consider the whole production chain, the macro-sector was worth 9.31% of Italy's GDP in 2004 and employed over 2.8 million people.

In general the situation in Italy's cultural industries encompasses both bright spots and shadow.

Table 9.1 Value added and jobs by sector in the chain of value creation in Italy (2004)

		Value added (m €)	Jobs (in thousands)	% VA of GDP	% Jobs in sector out of total jobs
Material culture	Fashion	38,024.2	1,112.6	3.04	4.59
	Industrial design and crafts	19,659.7	520.7	1.57	2.15
	Food and wine industry	5,054.8	125.1	0.40	0.52
Industry of content, Information and communications	Software	14,641.4	282.7	1.17	1.17
	Publishing	10,781.8	224.9	0.86	0.93
	TV and radio	4,070.8	89.4	0.33	0.37
	Advertising	2,405.8	64.9	0.19	0.27
	Film	1,929.8	37.6	0.15	0.16
Historic and artistic heritage	Cultural heritage	7,811.0	105.4	0.63	0.44
	Architecture	6,683.5	172.3	0.54	0.71
	Performing arts	5,186.2	120.2	0.42	0.50
	Contemporary ART*	357.2	15.0	0.03	0.06
Total		116,606.2	2,870.9	9.31	11.85

Sources: (Santagata 2009); our elaboration of data collected by Istituto G. Tagliacarne (Rome) Data: *Asterisk* our estimation

The Content Industries

If we look at the section we have called the content industries, the weaknesses are clear: compared to foreign competitors, they have little market share; entrepreneurial drive appears to be weak. The situation can be taken in at a glance

The content industries have relatively little weight in terms of added value or number of employees. A handful of the major manufacturing industries easily outstrips them. Although Internet is revolutionizing the sector, Italy's productive apparatus at the beginning of the third millennium was undersized compared to others in Europe. Its record industry was one-third the size of the French one, one-fifth of Germany's and one-sixth of Britain's; its video industry was half the size of France's or Germany's, one-quarter that of Britain's.

What is happening in a competitive national and international context, which in the 1990s saw a rise in investments in its most valuable production factors and the discovery of new talent, and to an even greater degree witnessed the growth of promotion and commercialization costs for media products in both the old and new distribution networks? The short answer is that Italian companies in these categories are falling behind or failing, to the point that they are leaving the market. (Richeri and Spada 2004, p. 691).

Italian cinema production is weak in terms of world market share (14% in 2004), and especially weak in the newly emerging digitally recorded sector. If we exclude co-productions, in the first 5 months of 2005 the United States produced 107 films, followed by Brazil (19), Japan (9), China (8), Great Britain (3) and France (3). By the beginning of June 2005, not a single digitally produced film had been made in Italy (European Cinema Yearbook 2006). In fact 2005 was a difficult year for Italian cinema. Compared to 2004, investments went down 24.6%; the number of productions from 96 to 68; government subsidies from 83.4 to 21.8 million euros (Ferrari 2006). In terms of trends, values seemed to be stagnating around the average values for the previous 10 years.

Italian television is divided between the private market and state television. Protected by a language barrier (breached by the appearance of satellite technology controlled by foreign media magnates), until 1990 it developed in an unregulated market, and is technologically backward. Cable and satellite links, which in other European countries have high annual growth rates, are low in Italy in comparison with the total volume of programs on the air. Commercial television, founded on the false idea that it is provided free, exists in a duopoly in contraposition to the pay-TV market. The state television channels, whose existence is justified by the need to provide a public service, have been drawn into a process of homologation and dumbing down to the level of the private networks, with the result that they are producing palimpsests that are virtually identical. The only important quantitative note is that Italian-produced original television series are usually popular with the public and represent a significant share of the total programs.

Publishing is a fundamental part of the new multimedia industry. The shopping circuit most used by Italian readers is still the small independent bookshop even though the competition from large multi-product chains and newsstands is making inroads. The problem is that Italy's statistics on reading are the worst in Europe. Product and process innovation is evolving rapidly with the input of digital technology and new multimedia publishers, forcing traditional companies publishing on paper to reorganize and modernize. But other European countries are more advanced than Italy in this sector as well.

The world market in videogames is currently approaching 40 billion dollars and overtaking even turnover from cinema attendance. In the early 1980s, two Japanese firms, Sega and Nintendo, were the world's leading producers of videogame consoles, when Sony and Microsoft also entered the market in game platforms (Barthélemy 2006). Although often scorned as an example of low-brow culture, the sector is important in economic terms, considering that the cost of developing a top range game can come to about 10 million dollars, similar to what it costs to produce a film, and commercial success is achieved only with sales of between 1 and 3 million units. A game can be developed on an autonomous platform or on a computer. The following are the principal players in the videogame market:

- The firms that *build the platforms,* which have a maximum life cycle of 5 years.
- *Independent publishers*, whose income comes from royalties obtained from sales of games; in general they are the ones who finance new ideas.
- Those who do the *research on game development*; they are responsible for conception and innovation and often work independently from publishers and producers.
- *Independent consultants,* working in all stages of the production process: testing, game design, communication, advertising, graphics, etc.
- *Distributors*, the intermediaries between shops, producers and publishers.

Given the variety of players participating in the production of a videogame, the lack of entrepreneurial initiative in Italy is disappointing. Although 24 million Italians play them on consoles, Italy produces no videogames. Mobile-phone games or the serious games played on PCs represent promising new markets. France, Britain and Germany are taking advantage of the new opportunities this market affords. Italy has a discreet edge in terms of widespread cellphone use, offset by a comparative delay in the use of personal computers.

The Entertainment Industries

The overall picture of the Italian performing arts industry is complex. A basic point of reference is a government body called *Fondo unico per lo spettacolo* (United Entertainment Fund), a public cornucopia now running out of resources and the cause of much distortion. The Fund (FUS) is run by the ministry of Culture and in 2006 disbursed 377.3 million euros. Of this sum, 47.8% went to opera, 17.9% to cinema, 16.6% to theater, 14% to musical events and the rest was shared between less important sectors. Similar, or even larger sums of public money are contributed by local government.

In the field of opera and symphonic music, Italy undoubtedly has an edge over other countries, which it pays a great deal to maintain. Transforming its opera companies into 13 private foundations for opera and symphonic music did little to balance budgets. It is in any case a sector in which the country's productions are certain to have influence throughout the world. We could say that "trade follows opera", that the growth in the use of the Italian language abroad is linked to music lovers reading opera librettos and the fact that Italian symphony orchestras offer culturally attractive programs.

Unlike its opera, Italian theater does not enjoy the international prestige that would allow the country to benefit, even in immaterial terms, from providing support. Public and ministerial subsidies and funding from local government, often without clear objectives, merely support what already exists. The 1990s seem to confirm a phenomenon that could already be seen emerging in the previous decades – greater growth in supply than in demand (Brosio and Santagata 1991; Trezzini 2004). There are two possible interpretations: the benign, but dispiriting one is that the imbalance is due to saturation in demand having been reached, rather than being a clarion call to democratizing the theater; the more cynical one suggests that much public funding (FUS spending on theater came to about 62 million euros in 2006) is handed out merely on the basis of a theater existing, on the principle of "You exist, therefore I will subsidize you".

Popular music is closely linked to the record industry which in 2006, according to statistics from Federazione dell'industria musicale italiana (FIMI), directly or indirectly employed 50,000 people. Italy's position in the record industry is also weak. None of the international music majors is Italian. In 2000 the Italian record industry's sales were 1.4% of the world total, compared to 7.7% for Britain, 6.6% for Germany and 4.6% for France. From the creative point of view, it is interesting to note that the Italian popular music market is less influenced by foreign production than its cinema. In fact, according to Pricewaterhouse Coopers, in 2006 the Italian repertory represented 51% of market share and was increasing. In Italy the major share of the digital market is represented by mobile telephones (67%), whose turnover (7.7 million euros) exceeds that for music downloaded from Internet (3.05 million euros).

Industrial Design and the Material Culture Industries

In this category Italy is on the threshold of developments that could be called epoch-making. At the moment the cultural and symbolic presence of its products on world markets is impressive. But what will the future of its cultural and industrial districts be when faced with the delocalization of production to countries with low labor costs? To what extent will Italy be able to guarantee generational succession for the great creative talents that made its fashion and furniture design famous?

In short, the shift from "made in Italy" to "styled in Italy" is going to require far-reaching structural, qualitative change and a high level of social creativity.

Industrial policy by itself is not capable of providing the answers needed. Culture must once more be at the center of all institutional development.

What Is at Stake

The impact of the cultural industries is a decisive factor both internationally and nationally.

International Impact

At the international level, the strength of its cultural industries is a decisive factor in creating and communicating a favorable image of a country's products and boosting sales. Cinema, music, design and the other arts are a showcase in which a country's outstanding products are made known to consumers throughout the world, whose choices are often the result of mental processes that intertwine cultural images of the past and present, of one sector and another. As early as 1912, United States Senator McBridge declared that trade followed films, underlining the importance of the success of Hollywood movies, first on an ideological level, imposing America's lifestyle, then on the commercial level, supplying the goods that feed that style (nowadays from Coca-Cola to sportswear to computer software).

On the international level, leadership in the cultural industries creates a continual flow of talent towards the country that is the front runner. This is essential for maintaining a high rate of creativity in the transition from one generation to the next. On the other hand, it is difficult to maintain a situation of equilibrium, because if a country's cultural industries are weak, this creates a brain drain towards more dynamic, more attractive markets. For instance, the immense industrial-design sector and the production of material culture (including architecture), together with opera and classical music, are the cultural flagship of contemporary Italy. In addition the country's cultural heritage and past cultural achievements attract creative talent and offer the places where creativity and tradition express the highest quality of life.

Social Impact

Cinema, like television, plays an important role in educating young people. Defending and reinforcing the cultural industries serves to defend and reinforce a nation's cultural identity.

Without solid cultural industries a country is exposed to invasions by other cultures. In the cinema market, in the decade 1990–2000, American films controlled between 46.7 and 70% of the Italian market; similar or even higher figures hold for other European countries and the Third World. Pay TV in Italy is in fact controlled by Sky and News Corp; videogames are imported; the majors in the record industry, although attentive to the taste of the Italian public, are in any case foreign multinationals. The term cultural invasion may be a bit too strong but the phenomenon is negative not only because it creates the premises for lifestyles that belong to other cultures being assimilated, but also because it interferes with the development of a distinctive national culture; the national culture is then too weak to produce cinema images and music of its own and original cultural models. Lacking the capacity to create myths of its own, a country loses its sense of identity. The process is reversible, but only in the long term and, as can be seen in the history of developing countries, the influence of a dominant culture, that of the colonizer, will continue to be deeply felt.

The counterpoint to cultural invasion is the positive concept of multiculturalism, which signifies respect for differences and an awareness that there is no single best identity, but many complementary ones. We can identify ourselves as citizens of the world and of our country and as belonging to one or more social groups (UNDP 2005, Chap. 5). Multiculturalism also expresses the capacity to self-correct no longer viable ethical values, such as the denial of women's rights or the refusal to allow people to participate in democratic processes.

In an era of renewed cross-border migration, cultural policies have a vital role in facilitating the social inclusion of newcomers. But in this instance, too, it is not going to be Renaissance or nineteenth-century culture that will create the conditions needed to reduce the distance between heterogeneous cultures from around the globe. It is the arts and cultural industries that speak a globally understood language, capable of making dialogue, reciprocal respect and shared communication of universal values possible. Cinema, Internet, music, design and contemporary art can unite, while the cultures of the past often appear to be in conflict with the phenomenon now known as globalization.

Economic Impact

The greatest threat to the economy of a country where the cultural industries are weak is the loss of opportunity. Such a country risks losing the train that could link its culture to modern technologies and new forms of expression. Those that from the start have been left behind in a world of growing profitability, such as that of the cultural and creative industries, will find it difficult to catch up. Those in the lead will be increasingly innovative and aggressive. While industrial design is an example of a success story for the Italian manufacturing industry, the country's cultural industries are struggling to keep abreast of international competition.

Universities and professional schools are not enough. Sound, images, the Internet have developed a new diversified, highly qualified and self-sustaining labor market. The production *filière* in every sector are the new schools for widespread, dynamic entrepreneurship.

High risk and high profits are often the basis of a monopolistic tendency or the emergence of an oligopolistic structure. This transformation, however, does not find in Europe an aggregation that would be sufficient to consolidate the emergence of powerful majors.

The cultural industries are a strategic sector for most countries yet lack specific corresponding institutions, such as a ministry of culture, that could bring to industrial, monetary, fiscal and sectorial policies, the attention inherent in an independent point of view.

Chapter 10
The Market in Contemporary Art

One of the sectors in which creative competition is fiercest is the contemporary visual arts. It is a sector that by definition produces culture. In an international market that is substantially private, with a significant volume of sales off the books, there are thousands of painters and sculptors seeking success. The prime condition for producing culture is obtaining market share, which means excelling in quality and the ability to sell symbolic and aesthetic values.

Italy is not the most important market in contemporary art in the world, yet the success stories of its best artists are an example of an important category of cultural production.

In general it can be said that the episodes in the story of contemporary Italian art would need to be staged in two acts. The first would relate the international success of twentieth-century artists. Lucio Fontana, Alberto Burri, Piero Manzoni, the Arte Povera group, Transavanguardia and some of the highly acclaimed talents of recent years, like Maurizio Cattelan and Vanessa Beecroft, are courted and held in high regard by museum directors and important collectors throughout the world.

The second act would depict young artists launching a poorly prepared assault on the hallowed strongholds of the art world. The task is not an easy one, their strategy and tactics are weak and success is dubious.

We can start from two observations. First, unlike the generations that preceded them, young Italian artists today are less successful than their peers in the United States, Britain, Germany, China and Japan. The second is that on the major international markets (London, Paris, New York), new generations of artists, for reasons that I will set forth below, succeed their predecessors more rapidly than in the past – what is implied by "generation" is a far shorter time span. The outcome is that in those markets the system is in full swing and can satisfy collector demand with new names and new styles. The young are important.

To understand how talented young people working in the Italian artistic tradition could be promoted, we need to take a step back and take a fresh look at two important aspects of the art market.

The first concerns the institutional profile of the labor market in the art world. A market of this type is rigidly segmented in specific positions; these are limited in

W. Santagata, *The Culture Factory*,
DOI 10.1007/978-3-642-13358-9_10,

number and conquering them is impeded by the people who occupy and defend them – successful artists, those who have already gained a foothold. For example the Gagosian Gallery which has locations in London, New York and Beverly Hills or Gallerie De Meo in Paris handle a limited number of artists because of the amount of work on communication and organization that marketing an artist entails. The art world is therefore a small, restricted, minimal space, fraught with competitive conflict, especially between the young, who want to emerge, and the old, who are going ahead with their creative productive activity.

It may seem paradoxical, and successful Italian artists are not willing to admit it, but when you speak to a gallerist in New York's Chelsea, London's Soho or the Latin Quarter in Paris, you realize that the international success of Arte Povera or the Transavanguardia was and continues to be such that it has overshadowed the work of the younger generation of Italian artists, obscuring their message and impeding their entry to the market. The fathers are eating their children.

There are economic reasons for all this: the current domination of the creation and the distribution phases in the chain of production of artistic value. The art market rewards those who invest in relational and in aesthetic-creative capital (Sacco 1998).

Relational capital is substantially the accumulation of relations with others working in the same system, what we now call networking. It involves forming connections whose value increases more than proportionally with each additional relation. If you do not dialogue with collectors and other artists, are not sought out by curators, are not visible, then you do not have connections and someone who is not connected is not in the picture (Santagata 2005).

Creative capital is instead the personal, compulsive, creative dimension of the individual artist's research. It requires neither contacts nor socializing. On the contrary, the search often involves study (perhaps at school), hard work and solitude.

Let us note here that these two forms of capital are distributed asymmetrically: the aesthetic-creative type is acquired by all generations and at any age, although it can be expressed very early in an artist's first work. It is the logical consequence of the natural distribution of artistic talent joined to personal commitment. But relational capital by definition belongs to artists who have been successful. A young person who sallies forth onto the market for the first time has no relational capital, which it is all the more important for an unknown artist to have, however, as the risk involved for others in the market, from dealers to collectors, is greater, given the uncertainty that surrounds the quality of works of art.

In Italy this asymmetry is particularly strong and penalizes young artists. If we wish to transmit the creative capital accumulated by older artists to future generations, we need to have a vast systematic series of possible ways of selecting young artists. Support for and promotion of the best young artists needs to become an actively pursued cultural offensive.

There are many policies that could help focus attention on young artists. The most important is a selection process art schools and academies can take part in. If today the core international markets are in New York, Paris, London and Berlin, it is there that the best art academies are to be found. And it is there, in those academies, that young artists first need to break into the art world. To make a name in those markets, they need to show that their preparation and technique are top-notch. They need to possess the means of artistic expression conventionally given recognition on the international scene in those metropolises. What we see is that young Americans who graduate from Parsons, Columbia University's Department of Art, and the Pratt Institute obtain recognition and begin meaningful careers. The same is true for young Britons who study at the Slade School of Fine Art, Royal College of Art, Saint Martins, and Goldsmiths. If a country's young artists want to be successful on international markets, they have to go to those cities, enroll in and attend those schools. This is the overall picture, because in the future there are sure to be artists like Maurizio Cattelan who manage to make a name for themselves worldwide; here what is at stake is an entire generation of young artists.

So what is involved is studying, and studying at the best schools. After all, haven't, for example, faculties of economics and medicine at Italian, Indian and Egyptian universities long been sending their best students to complete their studies at Cambridge, Harvard, or Chicago University? Isn't this what French stylists and fashion designers do when they send their most talented to study at London or New York's most creative schools? Of course, assisting someone to study abroad is a choice aimed specifically at obtaining a return. It does *not* mean being awarded a grant for a 4- or 5-month stay at the Italian Academy in New York. Nor does it mean getting a scholarship to stay in a place where the recipient will spend most of the time in isolation, with limited opportunities for networking. What it does mean is studying. Just as for other professions there are masters and doctoral degrees, the same should be true in the field of art. In exchange for financial aid, young people can be required to work seriously in internationally competitive schools. Let them become the best in the class where markets are strongest and most dynamic, and their likelihood of success will increase because good results at school are an important investment not only in creative capital, but in relational capital as well.

There are some who think that better solutions are to be found at home and that the country's academies of the fine arts could be resuscitated and transformed into centers of excellence. At the moment I doubt this is a viable alternative. The reasons are simple. Italy, for example, has about fifty state-supported or legally recognized academies of the fine arts and about fifty conservatories of music (cf. Table 10.1). Thousands of students graduate each year. The 2001 census showed that at least 80,000 Italians had received a diploma from an academy for the fine arts or a

Table 10.1 Advanced studies in art and music in Italy

Institute	Number
State academies of the fine arts	20
Private, officially recognized academies of the fine arts	25
National academy for the performing arts	1
National academy of dance	1
Conservatories	57
Private, officially recognized music institutes	22
Secondary schools for artistic trades	4

vocational high school of art. Over 300,000 graduated from a high school where they specialized in art or received a diploma from an institute of art. Despite this, a recent study on contemporary Italian art abroad (Sacco et al. 2005) found that Italy's young internationally successful artists can be counted on the fingers of one hand. What is happening? What isn't working? Fifty academies of art represent a considerable investment. Why aren't they consistently turning out a multitude of successful young artists?

The answer, which is neither an easy nor a conclusive one, is to be sought both in a judgment on the quality of Italy's schools and in the inefficiency of its world of art.

Academies of the Fine Arts

First the academies. They must learn to adapt to the ongoing evolution in the international art market. It is their task to identify from generation to generation what the dominant international convention in art is and get young students into tune with it.

Of course there are no universally held criteria for judging contemporary art and no absolute criteria, either. Success, veneration, criticism, acclaim, stricture are what historically have determined success or failure. In other words artistic judgment develops on the basis of men and women establishing social conventions which define what beauty, nature, civilization and the human condition are.

What then is the contemporary-art convention? It is the key for reading works of art, or a canon, in force at a given moment in history, within a given community, in a given place. It tells us how we should look at a work of art and allows us to judge to what extent it diverges from the established canon. It is a shared agreement on the qualitative aesthetic and social contents a work of art should have.

The contemporary-art convention is an informal one, in other words it is not written down or promulgated by a legal authority. The more I use a convention, the better I learn the code and the less it will cost me to read, accomplish or acquire a work of art. A convention, finally, is not a straightjacket, nor does it require homologation; it is a code that leaves each person free to express a personal way of thinking.

The construct of the contemporary-art convention not only serves to settle controversies between critics on the worth of individual artists and their work, but more importantly, it is a compass that makes it possible to navigate the seas of the international contemporary-art market. How can international success be achieved? Which market parameters are changing? What modifications in the art world's distribution and support systems will these changes bring about?

Economic science has nothing to say on the contents of the contemporary-art convention, but as a social science it studies how shared rules, i.e., conventions, are born, evolve and disappear. Its findings may be useful even for those who *make* contemporary art. We have no universal interpretative key, no yardstick, but we know how a convention functions and who controls it (at different times this could be artists, patrons, collectors, critics, museum directors). We know that once it has taken shape, a convention is widely shared because it reduces the costs of the risky decisions that those involved in art have to make, e.g., it reduces the margin of risk involved in investment by collectors or a curator's choices.

Two different levels of analysis will allow us to explore the contemporary-art convention in time and space.

The first concerns its content. It indicates the aesthetic canon of artistic quality. In the past the conventions of what represented quality in a contemporary work of art were "flatness", pop art, minimalism, using cheap and commonly available materials, the supremacy of concept. And today?

The second type of analysis in some ways concerns the conditions and restrictions that accompany and explain the emergence of a convention: direction of demand; the effects globalized markets and technology have on the production and distribution of art; the relation between a country's culture and an international, multicultural canon.

How far have we got? Put differently, a contemporary-art convention founded on an international standard is in the air, perhaps in the curricula of the world's best art academies, but has it been understood by academies in other countries? The impression is that the two models of conservation and production of culture are reflected in the divergence between traditional academies and the world's foremost schools of art. While the former aim to teach a discipline, transmitting artistic techniques and consolidated knowledge that will form a style, the latter are more oriented towards valorizing students' artistic intelligence. The former believe they have a grand tradition to bequeath to future generations; for international schools, success coincides with access to the art market, the ability to find an original way to develop the conventions of art perceived and valued by galleries, museums, critics and collectors. For traditional academies what is important is teaching anatomy and pictorial, sculptural, metal-working and engraving technique; international schools focus on interdisciplinary studies, work-study programs, courses on how markets work, marketing and the media.

I have said there are no definitive answers, yet we need to have a clear picture of what is happening. For example, it would be useful to have a system of rating art schools, indicating variations in their quality over the years. The more art comes to be considered a profession, the more relevant educating artists is. The school or academy becomes a strategic factor not only for the quality of each artist's work, but also for the artist's reputation. Rating schools of art, both public and private, is a delicate task, but one which needs to be carried out if we wish to complete a map of the risks the reputation a country's contemporary art is likely to face in the years to come.

The Italian Market and the Lack of Independent Centers

Like that of many other countries, Italy's world of art is strangely asymmetrical. On the one hand there are both outstanding institutions and museums of contemporary art, and competent, serious dealers and gallery owners. On the other, there is a dearth of organisms mediating between art galleries and museums, those that represent the formative, experiential fabric of young artists. Some independent art centers, such as Fondazione Pistoletto in Biella or *Kunsthalle*, could be called non-museum art centers but their role is to communicate young artists' work and contribute to circulating information and artists (Santagata 1998b). In some ways they are a means of networking, i.e. the exchange of ideas between artists, organizations and institutions, and policies which encourage accumulating relational capital. Centers of art can arrange for *curators from abroad* to visit Italy and become familiar with what is happening there (the Venice Biennale, museums of contemporary art, galleries, local networking). They can organize residence programs for *foreign artists* (commissioning work and arranging teaching fellowships in art academies) and for *teachers* from international art schools. They can stipulate contracts with suppliers of *international databases* so that they oversee the Italian component of the information web and provide centralized exhibition support to Italy's cultural institutes.

Even in the most private sphere of artistic production, contemporary visual art, producing culture is a political-institutional option whose future success is certain.

The Market and Contemporary-Art Cultural Districts: The Example of Beijing

Networking, the conventions of art, work-study programs for young artists, reduced information and transaction costs, production of creative emotions: all this happens and is multiplied in a contemporary-art cultural district. Throughout history certain cities have witnessed agglomerations of artists analogous to what we now call cultural districts (Florence, Rome, Venice, Paris, London, New York) yet nowhere has there been anything remotely like what is now happening in the Chinese megalopolis of Beijing.

The city's *Dashanzi Art District*, also called *Factory 798*, is in fact an outstanding example of a cultural district specializing in the production of contemporary art. It is a territorial system with artists' studios, galleries and small businesses, that has literally taken off in recent years, its success creating a strong market for contemporary Chinese art.

It is not difficult to predict what will happen: China will soon become one of the world's largest markets for contemporary art. The reasons are mainly economic ones – the law of large numbers. China is a market with 1.3 billion potential consumers, thousands of whom are very wealthy, and all that is needed is a bit of entrepreneurial initiative to make reputations and trigger commercial success on a scale that would be unthinkable in other countries' "small" markets. However, even with these large numbers, China cannot afford to make mistakes because, as we shall see, in the contemporary-art market the risk of speculative bubbles is clearly present.

Until recently work by Chinese artists was bought mainly by Europeans, Americans and collectors from Hong Kong, but when with the current economic boom Chinese collectors move into the market, they will flood in, they will arrive en masse, a sort of tsunami, and this will inevitably create enormous demand.

In overall terms, it could be said that in Beijing today there are relatively few galleries for a very large number of artists. "Many artists for few galleries" means that it is creativity, a mass of spontaneous self-fueling artistic production, that controls the market. The opposite, typical of mature markets like London or New York, is "many galleries for relatively few artists": normalization and standardization prevail; it is the market that controls art.

Obviously, the quality of the Beijing artists differs, but all of them, known or unknown, were born in the 1960s and 1970s. The birth of a cultural district is always something unexpected, impossible to plan. *Factory 798*, the original name of the Beijing art district, is said to have come into being as a confinement area, a location where it would be possible to exert political control over artists, who would incidentally be offered a place to work. Even today there are police at the entrance to the district. Yet much has changed in recent months and the district is now perceived in positive terms, helping the government to associate the modernization of the country with successful contemporary culture. Today busloads of tourists arrive to see what is happening. The *Danshanzi Art District* appears in guidebooks and on the pages of cultural events in Beijing. It has become fashionable to go there.

In it we find all the typical features of a cultural district:

- *Information circulates freely*. Imagine a hundred or so gallerists and art dealers, hundreds of artists, critics, art historians and curators who meet morning, noon and night to share information, talk over plans and discuss ideas on art and society. Add a few dozen foreign critics, curators and collectors who are visiting or have been invited to events that untiringly follow one another. Now add hundreds of working artists exhibiting in shows held in former factories. What you will have is a vital, vivacious agora of art.
- *The international dimension is fully achieved.* China is so large it could continue to be self-referential yet it has instead enthusiastically embraced other countries' experience. Everyone – artists, gallerists and organizers – are eager to speak to the world. Obviously in the Beijing art world, prices for artworks are in dollars or euros, not in Chinese currency. There are several international galleries in the district.
- *There is competition* between economic agents, yet there is also reciprocal trust and *cooperation*.
- *There is production of culture* thanks to the presence of the hundreds of artists who work there daily and exhibit in its galleries. The cultural atmosphere can be breathed, felt; there is spirit of identification with a unique place; there is creativity.
- Another extremely interesting aspect are the *art-market development services* that have been generated. These services, which allow artists, gallery dealers and collectors to compete on what is a difficult market include indoor and outdoor landscape design; graphic design; communications and television production;

Table 10.2 The Dashanzi art district in figures

Type of business	Number
Art galleries	82
Artists' ateliers (individual and collective; hundreds of artists are onwaiting lists)	54
Art-market services (communications, advertising, printing, digitalization, etc.)	31
Shops	12
Photography studios	2
Cafés and restaurants	8
Art spaces	17
Other	3

multimedia and Internet; organizing exhibits and cultural events; state-of-the-art photography studios; high-definition color printing and reproduction; public relations and advertising.

- *The district is on the move*. It is a powerful machine, creating synergies that increase the speed of the transformation it is undergoing. It works. And it is evolving: the first Beijing Biennale was held in 2003, the first Dashanzi International Art Festival in 2004; music and theater performances have also been organized. The district is growing by the day, engulfing other areas, such as *Factories 797* and *799*.
- The Dashanzi Art District, finally, is enlivened by *small boutiques, cafés and restaurants, bookshops* with a good selection of works on art history and criticism, and shops specializing in art objects. This gives it a vaguely European feel.
- In short it is a place where artists can find the stimuli they need to valorize their creativity and talent. While a few years back emerging galleries were the foundation on which the *Dashanzi Art District* was built, today world-famous galleries arrive and open 3,000-meter-square exhibition spaces. Naturally there is no lack of sponsors: Sony, Christian Dior, Toyota, etc. Decentralized, yet strategically located between the city center and the airport, the district is the lungs and heart of Beijing's creativity in art.
- Its statistics are impressive: over 200 art-related businesses and organizations currently work there (cf. Table 10.2).
- Of course there are things that need to be ironed out. The district is administered by a specially created body, the Beijing 798 Art Zone Administration Development Office, which responds more to the demands of the market than to those of art. With property values in the city spiralling upwards, there is pressure to construct new skyscrapers and dislodge artists. Beijing will perhaps have one directional center more and one creative district less. Time will tell.

The market in contemporary Chinese art is a bo-bo (bourgeois-bohemian) market, moving so rapidly that it cannot find the time to consolidate its advances. Speculation and incongruous prices may come as a nasty surprise to inexperienced collectors. Many instruments which are taken for granted in developed markets (selection, guarantees and rights) are still lacking but as we know, despite everything, the market in contemporary art continues to be a rebel system, a system with few rules.

Chapter 11
Producing Culture by Means of Museums

For dedicated defenders of the historic and artistic heritage, conserving cultural artifacts is the prime objective of public policy and thus represents a model that is even purer than that of the production and consumption of culture. In Italy, conserving and safeguarding art and culture is the categorical imperative of the art historian and of the Ministry of Culture's *Soprintendenze*, locally based authorities for the care of historic artworks and architecture, a legacy of a law enacted in 1939. The enjoyment and valorization of art are of secondary importance; after all, producing culture is not their job, almost as though creative activity and the generation of new ideas might somehow expose them to competition, turn them into vulnerable parts of a process, or unseat them as the high priests of culture.

Contrary to what is normally thought, the museum is an extraordinary mechanism for producing culture, especially if we allow it to be transformed into a multifunctional, democratic, free-access cultural center which promotes events and plays an active part in local development, and it is to this process that I will devote the final section of this chapter. I will not describe the museum as a cultural center's different potential spheres of cultural production, about which everything (and its opposite) has been said, but will instead attempt to set forth the economic and market prerequisites that facilitate its production of culture. The equation I have in mind is that in order to produce culture, a museum must develop a two-way link with its visitors, stimulating them to consume culture and being stimulated by them. The essential condition for this link is maximum access to what the museum has to offer, as otherwise elitism and social exclusion prevail, impeding that link with the territory, the local community and their development that is the second prerequisite. This is another instance of cross-fertilization: the museum becomes an agent in local development by promoting and implementing projects and new cultural products; the better urban and social conditions that ensue create the prerequisites for greater demand for culture.

W. Santagata, *The Culture Factory*,
DOI 10.1007/978-3-642-13358-9_11,

From Museum to Cultural Center

Like anything that conceals/reveals, the museum experiences continuous disequilibrium: there is always tension between its two functions – and within each function. Concealing means that works of art from the past and the contemporary period need to be conserved, safeguarded, cared for. Revealing means exhibiting, showing, rereading, evoking the hidden value of art. The artwork is hidden in a safe place, or at least that is the intention of those conserving it, and is revealed to those who want to see it. It is increasingly evident that the two operations are not separable and the boundary between them goes beyond museum exhibition spaces or the circle of visitors, users and consumers. In this sense, using a museum to produce culture is inevitably an action that coincides with valorizing a territory and its knowledge. If it is true that museums are the guardians of the passion of collectors who wish to prevent the dispersion of the works of art they have spent a lifetime collecting and transmit them to a community and a territory, rather than leave them to heirs who are uninterested in or insensitive to art, even in this founding act there is something greater than the simple sum of the works brought together. There is a link with a specific community. There is the wish to make an investment in order to offer pleasure and education to others. There is an attempt to keep the historic and artistic heritage alive and allow others to experience it.

In general the model of conservation per se, although an essential prerequisite, has outlived its usefulness: it costs a great deal, involves few and does nothing to advance the frontiers of knowledge and creativity. I feel the most vital tendency in recent decades has been the amplification of the museum's function and its transformation into a cultural center. Originally a place for collecting and exhibiting artworks, today, by doing historical research, organizing temporary exhibits, inventing cultural events and urban projects that involve the territory and its community, the museum has become a place of cultural production. Some of these functions are new and require structural changes. A museum crushed by the weight of its permanent collection, one that is not obtaining the fabulous income that most museums only dream of from the sale of tickets and services, will tend to develop an internal structure that is little oriented towards new functions: a large number of art historians and custodial staff and few experts on exhibiting, cultural events, marketing, communications, legal matters and intellectual property rights.

The passage from museum to cultural center, thus involves not only a rethinking of daily activities, but also forces the institution to rewrite its mission, comprised of programs, attention to a wide, diversified public, communicating a strong image, and participation in and promotion of cultural policy (Varine 2002; Santagata 2001a, b).

For the future, from the standpoint of experience, there are three questions that deserve particular attention: increasing the free admission area; decentralizing within the city and to surrounding towns; the passage from the museum as an institution that exists in isolation, to the museum as an institution that is integrated with its territory and is a co-agent in local economic and social development.

In Praise of Free Admission and Voluntary Contributions

In many countries, the question of free access is not "in". Today it is more fashionable to speak about the payment of flexible admission fees, designed to meet the needs of different categories of visitors. I would like, however, to summarize the positions in the debate as I am not fully convinced that we should not be seeking alternative solutions.

When I am standing on line, waiting to buy a ticket to a museum, I realize (with a twinge of pain) that entry fees are a way to ration consumption. Market logic decrees that those who pay get in. Museums in Italy, for example, cannot be accessed free. The hypothetical line of potential entrants is drastically cut in two: those willing to pay the set entry fee can enter, while *everyone else* remains outside.

The *everyone else* category deserves to be examined in further detail, as it includes both people whose demand is nil or even negative, and those with a *positive* demand, who would benefit in some way from consuming. This is the point. Is there any equitable, socially shared criteria that can justify excluding from a museum all those that would like to enter, but at a lower price than the one established?

The *ultraliberal* view, firmly anchored to an individualist and utilitarian vision of economic choices, is that a museum's budget, like that of a family, has to take into account current running expenses as well as fixed costs, say for installation. Liberal virtue – "There's no such thing as a free lunch" – thus coincides with covering total costs, no matter what happens. But inevitably something irreparable occurs, because the museum-enterprise cannot survive solely with its own resources. The costs covered by selling tickets represent a very small part of expenses, in general around 10–15% of the average cost per visitor. Faced with the dead end this leads to, those who back this approach will accept some variations: net costs, after entry fees have been deducted, can be covered using public funding, considering the cultural value of what is being subsidized; the alternative is to turn to private patrons, encouraged by suitable tax deductions.

The other approach is based on the principles of welfare economics. If the "private" accounts of each individual museum are not important and what matters is the accounts of society in general, the point of view from which the problems of financing a national museum system are seen changes radically. Let us imagine ranking potential visitors according to the benefits they could obtain. In first place we find those who place a high monetary value on entering the museum, followed in decreasing order, and according to their preferences, by all other visitors, down to those who assign zero value to doing so. Let us posit that overall social welfare is equal to the sum of individual benefits: it is clear that establishing a single admission fee, for example one identical to the average cost per visitor, excludes from consumption all those that deem that entry is worth less. Collective well-being decreases. Here the sum of unrealized benefits is a cost that can be ignored by the director of an individual museum, but not by society or by the ministry of culture. More specifically, the costs of the country's museum system should be set against benefits to individuals, adding on the additional benefits we could call *external*, those which stem from increased cultural consumption, ranging from the pleasure of living in an environment that is more sensitive to art, to bequeathing culture to future generations.

The first model is clearly structurally weak, in terms both of well-being and fairness. When we exclude a visitor who has a *reserve price* (i.e. an individual benefit) that is lower than the cost of admission (even if we only mean the price reduction that comes with purchasing an annual entry card), we are making an unwise economic decision as we forgo achieving a positive benefit at a cost that tends to approach zero. In fact the cost of having one *additional* visitor (what economists call marginal cost) is negligible: an imperceptible increase in cleaning and security expenses, insurance and heating/air-conditioning costs, and not much else. For decades, the theory of nearly non-existent marginal costs has been the strongest argument in favor of free admission, in Great Britain as in Italy, with public funding used to cover the difference between revenue (negligible) and total costs.

But there is more to it. When subsidies cover 80–90% of costs, what sense does it make to exclude potential visitors? To put it bluntly, why should that 90% be bestowed on those who are willing to or who *can* pay the admission fee and *not to everyone*? What criteria of distributive justice do we wish to apply?

The reasons set forth do not intend to evade the problem of financing. If the cost of one additional visitor is virtually nothing, total costs for salaries, maintenance and creating and arranging a collection weigh heavily on museum budgets. The difference between income and expenditure has to be covered in one way or another, and an important contribution is made by the visitors themselves, many of whom set a high positive economic value on seeing the museum. Failing to accept their willingness to pay is a luxury no country can afford. The "pay what you wish" system used by many museums in the U.S. and U.K. seems to work, both in terms of efficiency and fairness (Santagata and Signorello 2000).

Here then is a modest proposal directed at maximizing the general welfare: *free admission plus voluntary contributions*. Admission costs nothing, but people are asked to make a voluntary contribution. The museum's deficit, calculated as the difference between revenue and total costs, would be covered in three ways. With the first, the museum accepts visitors' willingness to make a voluntary contribution. The second uses the net profits from sales through ancillary commercial services (bookshops, cafés, merchandising, copyright on reproductions). The remainder would be financed by the state or by the private sector, through donations and sponsorship.

If what happened in the U.K. is any indication, once admission is free, there should be a considerable increase in demand. In the U.K. the number of *extra* visitors to national museums increased by approximately 29 million between 2001 (the year the Labour Party decided to adopt a free admission pricing policy) and 2005. In Italy, a country where admission fees are set, according to the National Bureau of Statistics (ISTAT), in 1993, 77 Italians out of 100 had not visited a museum or a temporary exhibit during the year. There has since been a slight decrease in non-users: for 2000 the figure was 71. Much work has to be done.

In Praise of Decentralization and Democratization

The other aspect of drawing up admission policies that actively promote democratization of museum access is decentralization. The two are obviously closely connected, as democratizing access cannot be seen only in economic terms. The spatial dimension is equally important: it consists in bringing the museum where it has never been before.

There are many different ways to decentralize. Each museum needs to have a project which includes a wide variety of events. These could concern schools to increase involvement of the student public: young people as the target audience of new cultural activities and edutainment. They could involve producing a film, a travelling exhibition, virtual exhibitions, courses and theatre productions. Each of these, as we will see in the next section, has an important influence on a country's image and economy.

In Praise of the Museum as a Co-agent in Economic and Social Development

I have explained why, in my opinion, a museum's participation in local development is a source of and stimulus to cultural production. I will now explore the main reasons why a museum should contribute to local economic and social development.

- *It creates a collective image and identity.* A museum, with its art collection and cultural activities, transfers its image to the territory where it is located. Image is an economic good and can be reproduced and spent in different markets. An image has the economic value of the reputation that supports it and continually enriches it with creative and innovative input.
- A strong image appeals to people and becomes something with which they can identify. They identify with it because they want to share what the image represents in terms of good taste, artistic sense, historic heritage or cultural values. But when people identify with a particular symbol, a process of differentiation from other values is set in motion. Clearly, a cultural heritage is a source both of identification and differentiation. The latter has wide-ranging effects, for example in markets where product differentiation is essential for success. What I mean is that even sectors not directly connected to museums, such as the tourist industry or industrial design or the artisan sector, can benefit from a community's or territory's cultural-heritage image. The optimum benefit is obtained if the construction of image and identity is technically linked to developing and strengthening something that is visible and defendable – a collective brand name.
- *It produces culture by creating jobs and wealth.* As an economic structure, a museum has an important economic impact on local economy. The effects of a museum's economic activity can be direct, indirect or induced.

- The direct ones concern both supply and demand. A museum supplies jobs both to skilled workers (e.g. restorers, curators) and unskilled ones (e.g. custodial staff). It boosts real-estate values in its area, a boon to those who have residential or commercial property there. It stimulates related productive sectors, i.e. accessory services such as publishing, the manufacturing and merchandizing of objects to be sold to visitors, and mounting temporary exhibits.
- The indirect ones are principally those related to attracting tourism, in situations where tourist consumption of hotel and restaurant services and the goods of the local material culture and artisan sector show a profit. We know that tourism produces costs in terms of congestion, and sometimes, as can happen with one-day visitors, increases the city's expenditure for sanitation, public transport, etc. without producing income. Yet tourism, including congresses connected to events a museum as cultural center can organize, is a vital source of income for the local community. As a tourist destination, the museum becomes the heart of the cultural tourism industry.
- The induced ones are more hidden but are equally significant: a film, a television series, a school for restorers linked to the museum's permanent collection.
- *It is a source of professional training.* The human capital present in a museum is continually enriched through experience and can be accumulated by each new generation. In the cultural sector, learning on the job is among the most relevant forms of training. This, obviously, is increasingly so the less schools and art academies are able to transmit creativity and artistic knowledge.
- *It is a repository of traditional culture and know-how.* Local businesses can trace original sources of creativity through the museum's communication systems and archives. There are instances of outstanding interaction between a museum and a company, the former serving as the historical memory of the latter. In districts where material goods are produced, it is not unusual for small businesses to turn to museum archives to research traditional ceramics, cutlery, art glass, clothing or fabrics and use what they learn to relaunch contemporary production.
- *It is an element in urban and regional development policies.* The museum and its multiple functions can help local economic and social forces to achieve the priority objectives in development projects. There are several ways this can happen:

  (a) *If development means integration between cultures* in an age of migration and multiculturalism, shows, festivals, events and theatre performances are opportunities for encounter, the exchange of ideas and increasing reciprocal understanding. The museum per se is an exceptional means of social inclusion because it is naturally open to a comparison between different styles, languages and cultures, moving people towards dialogue and away from conflict and incomprehension.

  (b) *If development means generating income and jobs* by requalifying an urban area, the active presence of a museum can be a prime support. What has been done in cultural districts in cities in the United States, briefly described in Chap. 5, is the clearest example. These metropolitan cultural districts have shown how local business resources can be mobilized to supply services and material culture in the field of art. There are many U.S. and Canadian cities with cultural districts – from Boston to Toronto, from Baltimore to Pittsburgh and Houston – and often a district has over 100 current or planned projects of cultural development. In Great Britain the idea of the cultural district has been seen as a priority, both in theory and practice, since what was done in Glasgow in the 1980s.

Planning and building an urban cultural district, salvaging factories or unused areas not targeted for specific purposes, makes it possible to invent new sites for the creation and consumption of culture, among which museums, given their rich architectural qualities, constitute the point of maximum attraction.

In principle the metropolitan cultural district can satisfy two demands: the external demand of tourism and the internal demand of residents for a better quality of life.

(c) *If development means systematically using a city's cultural resources,* there are numerous advantages in creating a museum district. Not all of these have been fully exploited in Vienna, Berlin (and Europe in general), even when some form of museum district exists.

A move towards districtualization is an important contribution to local economic development. Its salient characteristics include the following five requisites: (1) spatial concentration of museums; (2) links with the local territory's social and cultural history; (3) a unifying theme so that despite diversity, the contents of the museums' collections are the expression of a single source of inspiration; (4) the existence of organizational hierarchies dedicated to a unified policy expressed through methods based on orientation and persuasion; (5) an international vocation.

Let us take Torino's Sabauda Gallery as an example (Santagata 2003a, b). Museographic innovation there consisted in identifying a model for exhibiting cultural artifacts that was very close to what had been done in other cultural districts. In fact although the House of Savoy's collections belong to several small to medium-sized museums, they can now be presented to the public in a unitary context rather than in isolation. This reinforces their appeal and communicative power, to the point that they have become a consolidated logo, a brand name in which the city can invest to further its international reputation and develop induced resources in the tourism and hotel sectors.

This innovation goes counter to the trends seen in the last few decades, which have tended towards super-specialization of museum vocations and contents, in other words a search for increasingly accentuated single-theme divisions: the Sabauda increasingly a royal picture gallery, the Egyptian Museum more and more a monument to itself. The formula of the museum district is the opposite of such policies of specialization, pursued as a way of winning the competitive struggle between one city and one museum and another. It counters this trend with the idea of a historical museum block, the cohesive, living representation of a territory and all the intellectual energies that have made it excellent.

Although the idea of districts is an appealing one, in Italy it has continually met with major obstacles along the road to being put into practice, principally, I believe, for institutional reasons. The ownership rights to parts of collections were widely dispersed during the last century between *Soprintendenze*, municipalities, non-profit bodies, foundations, universities and academies for the fine arts. In terms of rational behavior, this structure based on property rights oriented the evolution of local cultural systems towards super-specialization. The incentives to and the limits on action entailed in these rights, compelled each responsible party to devote itself exclusively to its own interests. It could not have been otherwise, as the message implicit in institutional regulations was this: specialize, invest in yourselves, compete with all others, defend your own image, increase your own fame, obtain more financial aid for your own collections. Competition between institutions is not necessarily negative, but in this case it weakened the higher value of promoting the group as a whole. What was seen is a classic case of path dependency, which shows how fundamental institutional starting points are in defining the way development proceeds in many cultural systems.

The concept of the museum district therefore moves towards recomposing the local historical and artistic culture and encouraging its collective development.

Chapter 12
Conclusions: A White Paper on Creativity and the Production of Culture

One need only glance at the Internet pages describing the politico-administrative structure of many developing countries to realize how much institutional responsibility for the production chain of art and culture has been dispersed between a plethora ministries, departments, art schools, universities, conservatories, chambers of commerce, local bodies, public associations and bank foundations. This holds true even for many developed countries. If to this we add the contribution of the private and non-profit sectors, we notice immediately how, at least in terms of providing orientation and political stimulus, the ministry for the cultural heritage and activities has left the lion's share of the production of culture to other institutions. These countries do not lack ministries for the protection of their cultural heritage. What they lack are ministries for the production of culture.

Taking Italy as an example, what we see is a manifestation of both strength and weakness. The ministry for the cultural heritage and activities is stronger because it is faithful to its original purpose – the custody, care and safeguarding of the country's cultural patrimony. In fact Italy's entire history from 1974 to the present is the story of the pre-existent structure. From the local *Soprintendenze* to the central offices, its work has focussed principally on surveillance, custody, restoration and conservation. Although new general administrative divisions were recently set up, such as one for contemporary art and architecture and others, like the ones for cinema and live performances, have existed for a number of years, it would be unusual for a regional authority (*Soprintendenza*) to be actively involved in the production of material culture, to show interest in fashion, for example, or the wine and gastronomic culture of the Piedmont's Langhe or Tuscany's Chianti regions. And it is even harder to imagine a locally based authority concerned with developments in videogames or their pirated counterparts, digital diffusion of music, mega-fusions between Internet, the entertainment and information industries, free digital copying (downloading) and the countermeasures taken by the record industry's majors to block free access to music via Internet.

This kind of ministry, whose identity is clear and whose name is internationally recognized in the sphere of safeguarding the country's cultural heritage, lacks muscle when it comes to the supply chain of cultural production. The sphere of

W. Santagata, *The Culture Factory*,
DOI 10.1007/978-3-642-13358-9_12, © Springer-Verlag Berlin Heidelberg 2010

public action has expanded and the concept of culture has come to encompass all forms of civilization; therefore new, interconnected sectors have come into play, from the creative industries to the production of culture on Internet. Globalization of markets and the worldwide spread of ICTs have oriented consumers preferences, creating a demand for new experiential and digital products. The conception and distribution phases, as was pointed out, have become the ones which determine the supply chain of cultural offerings, while conservation and custody/care are now simply two steps in the series, and not even the ones that are crucial to achieving a strategic position. New subjects are emerging as are new cultural mediators between production and consumption, specifically *precepteurs* who help distributors orient, and sometimes limit, public taste (Benghozi 2006).

A twofold problem has arisen. The first facet is that of defining priorities, the second concerns cultural orientation and coordination, as different needs may give rise to conflicts of interest, not only in terms of distribution (what weight should be given to various sectors in allocating public resources), but also regarding directional responsibility (who makes decisions in various sectors and in the different phases of the chain, who arbitrates in conflicts between cultural sectors) and institutions (who regulates intellectual property rights, especially in the new fields of digital cultural production). It has become imperative to have a comprehensive, full-range vision of cultural production. How can we guarantee cultural diversity and tolerance when we recognize new means of expression and avoid allowing the dominant culture to become invasive?

The departments of other ministries that deal with cultural production do so without the sensitivity and historic background required. Artisanship, industrial design, fashion, the cultural industries, for example, are sectors of great economic relevance for which there is no global, systematic cultural vision. Their valorization is prevalently industrial and commercial and this diminishes their cultural significance.

Few countries have ever had a ministry responsible for the production of culture, a comprehensive expression of global interest in the production of culture and its valorization. Rarely do we find a country with a ministry prepared to invest resources to transmit their parents' creativity to future generations.

The paradox is that even a country such as Italy, whose name is a byword for culture, should have come through the twentieth century with a series of ad hoc ministers of culture. Spadolini, appointed in 1974, was the first to head the Italian Republic's Ministry in charge of safeguarding the country's cultural and environmental heritage. It was a ministry that was created late, after 20 years of parcelling out responsibility to a host of government departments, from public works to education. It is a ministry that has turn out to be, as one government succeeded another, an organism whose shape and size were elastic: at one time or another it was responsible for sports, tourism, the theatre, cinema, the environment, publishing, and safeguarding intellectual property rights. The final assemblage responded to the dictates of party politics and the spoils system and whenever coherence and greater openness to the universal dimension of culture were called for, the phantoms of the fascist era or of Big Brother were inaptly evoked. The ministry for culture therefore had to cut out for itself a role in conservation that only slowly evolved into the current political structures codified in the new law safeguarding the country's cultural heritage.

And yet the new frontier is clearly identifiable: producing culture, comprehensively promoting creativity, backing artistic creation, increasing access to culture by reducing access costs, democratization, an active presence in the fields of communications and information technology, setting the country on the road to a knowledge society, assisting the development of the cultural and creative industries and cultural tourism, improving the quality of professional and academic courses, reaching and exceeding the magic 1% of the public budget, or rather public expenditure, earmarked for culture. Without becoming involved in the argument over the pros and cons of what has been called the invention of cultural politics (Urfalino 2004), there is a clear need for a unified institutional structure for the production of culture and this need can realistically be met, without either scandals or ideological preclusions.

From Now to 2025

"If I were the Minister of Culture..." we sometimes fantasize, I would produce a green book on creativity and producing culture. There'd be a work group to draw up a scenario that would stimulate and open nation-wide debate... a scenario that could project my country into a prominent position in the future in a society based on knowledge, innovation and creativity. The green book would point the way to a finish line that is not very near, because, as we have seen, some creative processes take a generation, but is not very far away, because competing countries around the world are not standing still and we have to make up for delays in a relatively brief period of time. Thus a great deal of work is going to have to be done to regulate the production of creativity and culture and establish clear-cut methods for evaluating social consequences in the next 20 odd years.

Let us therefore imagine a process that will get us to 2025 and beyond, enabling us to construct a country that will be culturally open and creative. To do this, the green book should both expose present-day lacks, inefficiency and backwardness (many of them briefly described in this volume), and indicate what questions the debate on transforming the country in the next quarter century should consider. Through the auspicious success of its creative industries and talented individuals, the country, within the limits of its historical capacity, will try to increase its influence in the world and consolidate its positions in the markets in culture and knowledge. Culture, as we have seen, is a value that is simultaneously symbolic and economic, capable of attracting talented individuals that wish to live and work in a place. This is a crucial point: the conservation model attracts tourists, not artists, cultural entrepreneurs and those who produce knowledge. If all this can be achieved, The country will be more open and tolerant, recognized by other nations not only for the beauty of its historic and natural sites, but also for the quality of life in its cities and its "culture factories".

Within the framework of being open to cultural production that I have attempted to sketch, certain policies emerge as priorities. I have tried to give a picture of the malaise and the expected fruits of production of culture in the sectors which are most delicate and most indicative of what is to come: from material culture, fashion and industrial design, to the cultural, creative and entertainment industries; from the historic and artistic heritage to contemporary art.

The green book will have to start from a review of what exists to stimulate debate and indicate what points have to be corrected and which sectors need to be developed and given political priority.

Priorities for 2025

The green book should deal with certain priorities. I will briefly mention what they are. The aim of these conclusions is in fact simply to focus attention on the problem of creativity and culture, without dealing in a systematic way with all the issues they involve.

- *Producing culture.* The first priority is to produce culture. This requires a far-reaching political program which would redefine individual and collective incentives for artists, public operators and entrepreneurs. The material costs do not appear to be excessively high, while the organizational and political ones are enormous. In the world's globalized economy, sectors like contemporary art, music, the cinema, publishing, television, and the design and the material culture industries constitute a country's creative system. It is the people who work in these sectors, together with those working in scientific and technologically innovative fields, that will define the creative image of the country in the twenty-first century and constitute its human capital. Strengthening interaction with the world economy sends the negative message of continuing dependence and subordination, failure to capitalize on our culture and what is attractive in it. The questions raised by digital culture and Internet have to coexist in this framework with a sensible approach to intellectual property, copyright and collective brand names.
- *Investing in human capital.* The second priority on our list, but not in order of importance, is investing in human capital. It is a choice that has to be made if our culture is to be conserved and transmitted to new generations. Although education systems around the world differ in quality, the ability to transmit knowledge and creativity on-the-job is of great value. This world of practical and theoretical experience, human and intellectual relationships, and tacit knowledge is what cultural districts or clusters have always done best. Schools should be more open to this sort of direct experience as this would make them more competitive in

relation to the methods that other countries, in particular the U.S. and U.K., have adopted to achieve excellence. Teachers, artists, artisans, designers, entrepreneurs, writers, musicians, engineers and scientists – all those who work in the world of creative production – should be systematically incentivated to open their offices and ateliers to young people and transmit the theory and practice of their vocations to them through direct experience.

- *Reducing the cost of access to culture.* This priority is especially relevant to young people, in the context of a gradually aging population. High prices limit consumption, depress the demand for culture, and favor manifestations which are only seemingly free, such as private television networks. Another politically relevant issue is working out a system that combines voluntary contributions with free admission to museums and freedom of access or global licensing for reading books, watching films and listening to music on Internet.
- *Offering a quality product to keep up with world markets.* Finally, offering a high quality cultural and creative product is the best protection from the competition, sometimes unfair, developing on the international market. This means holding onto market share by offering products and services whose qualitative content is increasingly better. Our best defence in limiting the negative effects of competition on production costs is to respond with creativity.

A green book that would mobilize the best minds in all sectors in the worlds of art and culture could represent a first step in the direction of a new cultural policy, not only for some developed country, but also for all developing countries with an unsurpassed cultural heritage that are experiencing similar difficulties in the transition from a conservation model to one of cultural production.

Although safeguarding, care and conservation are part an integral part of the production of culture, they must allow a country's creativity, which is struggling to compete on world markets, to breathe. My hope is that reallocating resources according to the underlying idea in "a bit more ministering to producing culture, a bit less ministry for the cultural heritage" will in the near future allow newly modernized countries to live up to the impressive historic traditions of their past.

References

Adorno, T. W., & Horkeimer, M. (1947). *Dialectic of enlightement*. Amsterdam: Querido.

Amabile, T., & Tighe, E. (1993). Questions of creativity. In J. Brockman (Ed.), *Creativity* (pp. 7–27). New York: Simon and Schuster Touchstone Books.

Arnault, B. (2000). *La passion créative, entretiens avec Y*. Plon, Paris: Messarovitch.

Bagnasco, A. (1988). *La costruzione sociale del mercato*. Bologna: Il Mulino.

Barrère, C., & Santagata, W. (2005). *La Mode. Une économie de la créativité et du patrimoine, à l'heure du marché*. Paris: La documentation Française.

Barthélemy, V. (2006). *La conception de jeux vidéos, mimeo C.R.G.* Paris: Ecole Polytechnique.

Baumol, W., & Bowen, W. (1966). *Performing arts: The economic dilemma*. Cambridge, MA: Twentieth Century Fund.

Becattini, G. (Ed.). (1987). *Mercato e forze locali. Il distretto industriale*. Bologna: Il Mulino.

Benghozi, P.-J. (2006). Mutation et articulation contemporaines des industries culturelles. In X. Greffe (Ed.), *Création et Diversité au miroir des industries culturelles* (pp. 129–152). Paris: La Documentation française.

Benghozi, P.-J., & Santagata, W. (2001). Market piracy in the design-based industry: economics and policy regulation. *Economie Appliquée, 3*, 121–148.

Benhamou, F. (2000). *Léconomie de la culture*. Paris: La Découverte.

Benjamin, W. (1936). L'oeuvre d'art à l'ère de la reproduction mécanique. *Zeitschrift fur Sozialforchung*, I, Jahrbuch V.

Bobbio, L. (1990). La politica dei beni culturali. In B. Dente (Ed.), *Le politiche pubbliche in Italia* (pp. 111–116). Bologna: Il Mulino.

Boden, M. A. (1991). *The creative mind, myths and mechanisms*. New York: Basic Books.

Bodo, C., & Spada, C. (Eds.). (2004). *Rapporto sull'economia della cultura in Italia 1990–2000*. Bologna: Il Mulino.

Bourdieu, P. (1971). Pour une économie des biens symboliques. *L'Année sociologique, 22*, 49–126.

Bourdieu, P. (1992). *Les règles de l'art*. Paris: Editions du Seuil. English edition: Bourdieu, P. (1996). *The Rules of Art: Genesis and Structure of the Literary Field* (trans: Susan, E.). Stanford, CA: Stanford University Press.

Bourdieu, P. (1994). *Practical reason: On the theory of action*. Stanford, CA: Stanford University Press. 1998.

Brosio, G., & Santagata, W. (1991). *Rapporto sull'economia delle arti e dello spettacolo*. Torino: Edizioni della Fondazione Giovanni Agnelli.

Bryant, W., & Throsby, D. (2006). Creativity and the behavior of artists. In V. Ginsburg, & D. Throsby (Eds.), *Handbook on the economics of art and culture*. Series "*Handbooks in*

economics", General Editors K. Arrow and M.D. Intriligator, North Holland, Amsterdam: Elsevier Science
Caves, R. E. (2000). *Creative Industries, trad.it. L'industria della creatività: economia delle attività artistiche e culturali*. Milano: ETAS.
Chomsky, N. (1968). *Language and mind, trad.it. Mente e linguaggio, in Saggi linguistici* (Vol. III). Torino: Boringhieri. 1969.
Creplet, F., Dupouet, O., & Vaast, E. (2003). *Episteme or practice? Differentiated Communitarian Structures.* in Biology Laboratory in Communities and Technology (Eds.), The Netherlands: Kluwer Academic Publishing.
Cuccia, T., Marrelli, M., & Santagata, W. (2008). Collective trademarks and cultural districts: the case of San Gregorio Armeno, Naples. In P. Cook & T. Lazzeretti (Eds.), *Creative cities, cultural clusters and local economic development*. Cheltenham: Edward Elgar.
Cuccia, T., & Santagata, W. (2004). Collective property rights and sustainable development: The case of the pottery cultural district in Caltagirone, Sicily. In E. Colombatto (Ed.), *Companion to property rights economics* (pp. 473–488). Cheltenham: Helgar Elgar.
Dacia Viejo, R. (2007). Conflict and the deliberate destruction of cultural heritage. In H. Anheier & Y. R. Isar (Eds.), *Conflicts and tensions. The culture and globalization series 1* (pp. 241–252). London: Sage.
Damasio, A. R. (1994). *Descartes error: emotion, reason and the human brain*. New York: G.P. Putnam's Sons.
DEPS, Departement des Etudes, de la Prospective et des Statistiques. (2006), "*Aperçu statistique des industries culturelles*", France.
Elster, J. (1996). Rationality and the emotions. *The Economic Journal, 106*, 1386–1397.
Emiliani, A. (1974). *Una politica dei beni culturali*. Torino: Einaudi.
European Cinema Yearbook. (2006). Downloadable: http://www.mediasalles.it/yearbook.htm.
Ferrari, P. (2006). *I dati della produzione italiana 2005*. Australia: ANICA Informa.
Fiorentino, P., Friel, M., Marrelli, M. & Santagata, W (2010). Cultural commons and cultural communities: The case studies of Milan designers and Italian futurists artists. In Working Papers. n. 02/2010, Ebla Center. Retrived from http://www.css-ebla.it.
Florida, R. (2002). *The rise of the creative class: And how it's transforming work, leisure, community and everyday life*. New York: Basic Books.
Forst Kumpf, H. A. (1998). *Cultural districts handbook: The arts as a strategy for revitalizing our cities*. USA: Americans for the Arts.
Gay, A. (1998). Selezione ed affollamento. In W. Santagata (Ed.), *Economia dell'Arte*. Torino: UTET.
Goleman, D. (1997). *Emotional intelligence*. New York: Bantam Books.
Harris, M. (1977). *Cannibal and kings. The origins of culture. trad.it. Cannibali e Re*. Milano: Feltrinelli.
Hopkirk, P. (1980). *Foreign devils on the silk road. The search for the lost treasures of Central Asia*. P. Hopkirk©.
Horvath, S. (1999). Economic modelling of creative behavior. *Society and Economy, 4*, 1–11.
Howkins, J. (2001). *The creative economy: how people make money from ideas*. New York: The Penguin Press.
Jalil Moreno, Y., Santagata, W., Tabassum, A. (2005). Cultura Materiale, diversità culturale e sviluppo economico sostenibile. *Sviluppo Locale*.
Jameson, F. (1984). Postmodernism, or the cultural logic of late capitalism. *New Left Review, 146*, 59–92.
Hall, P. (1998). *Cities in Civilization: Culture, Technology and Urban Order*. London: Weidenlfed and Nicolson.
Hall, P. (2000). Creative Cities and Economic Development. *Urban Studies, 37*, 639–649.
Kris, E., & Kurz, O. (1934). *Legend, myth, and magic in the image of the artist. A historical experiment.* New Haven, CT: Yale University Press. 1979.
Legrenzi, P. (2005). *Creatività e Innovazione*. Bologna: Il Mulino.

Leon, P., & Galli, G. (2004). Cambiamento strutturale e crescita economica del settore culturale. In C. Bodo (Ed.), *Rapporto sull'economia della cultura in Italia 1990–2000*. Bologna: Il Mulino.

Magnatti, P., Ramella, F., Trigilia, C., & Viesti, G. (2005). *Patti territoriali. Lezioni per lo sviluppo*. Bologna: Il Mulino.

Marshall, A. (1890). *Principles of economics*. London: Macmillan.

Marshall, A. (1919). *Industry and trade*. London: Macmillan.

Mossetto, G. (1993). *Aesthetics and economics*. Dordrecht: Kluwer.

OECD. (2005). *Culture and local development*. Paris: OECD.

Panofsky, E. (1939). *Studies in Iconology. Humanistic Themes in the Art of the Renaissance*. Oxford: Oxford University Press.

Paris, T. (2004). Industries culturelles et mondialization. In T. Montbrial & P. Moreau Defarges (Eds.), *Ramses 2003, Les grandes tendences du monde*. Paris: Dunod.

Polanyi, M. (1958). *Personal knowledge. Towards a post critical philosophy*. London: Routledge. 1998.

Polanyi, M., & Prosch, H. (1975). *Meanings*. Chicago, IL: The University of Chicago Press.

Richeri, G., & Spada, C. (2004). Audiovisivi, Introduzione. In C. Bodo (Ed.), *Rapporto sull'economia della cultura in Italia 1990–2000*. Bologna: Il Mulino.

Sacco, P. L. (1998). La selezione dei giovani artisti nei mercati delle arti visive. In W. Santagata (Ed.), *Economia dell'arte*. Torino: Utet.

Sacco P. L., & Pedrini S. (2003) *Il distretto culturale: mito o opportunità?* " Working Papers, EBLA CENTER, Dipartimento di Economia, Università di Torino

Sacco, P. L., Santagata, W., & Trimarchi, M. (2005). *L'arte contemporanea italiana nel mondo*. Milano: Skira.

Salais, R., & Storper, M. (1995). *Les mondes de production*. Paris: Editions de l'Ecole des Hautes Etudes en Sciences Sociales (Editions de l'EHESS).

Santagata, W. (1998a). Propriété intellectuelle, biens culturels et connaissance non cumulative. *Réseaux, 88–89*, 65–75.

Santagata, W. (1998b). *Simbolo e Merce*. Bologna: Il Mulino.

Santagata, W. (2000). Distretti Culturali, Diritti di Proprietà e Crescita Economica Sostenibile. *Rassegna Economica, 1–2*, 31–62.

Santagata, W. (2001). Cultura come bene idiosincratico, economia creativa e distretti culturali. *Economia della Cultura*.

Santagata, W. (2001b). *Produrre cultura II*. Torino: Celid.

Santagata, W. (2002). Cultural districts, property rights and sustainable economic growth. *International Journal of Urban and Regional Research, 26*, 181–204.

Santagata, S. (2003a). *I Distretti Culturali Museali. Le Collezioni Sabaude di Torino*. Torino: Istituto Fondazione A. Gramsci.

Santagata, W. (2003b). *The value chain of the cultural production, lecture in post graduate course 'Cultural Projects for Development'*. Turin: ILO.

Santagata, W. (2004). Creativity, fashion, and market behaviour. In D. Power & A. J. Scott (Eds.), *The cultural industries and the production of culture* (pp. 75–90). London: Routledge.

Santagata, S. (2005). Indagine sull'arte contemporanea italiana a Londra. In P. L. Sacco, W. Santagata, & M. Trimarchi (Eds.), *L'arte contemporanea italiana nel mondo*. Milano: SKIRA.

Santagata, W. (2006). Cultural districts and their role in developed and developing countries. In V. Ginsburg, D. Throsby, K. Arrow, & M. D. Intriligator (Eds.), *Handbook on the economics of art and culture* (Handbooks in economics). North Holland, Amsterdam: Elsevier Science.

Santagata, W. (Ed.). (2009). *Libro bianco sulla creatività in Italia* [White Paper on Creativity in Italy]. Milano: Università Bocconi Editore (Retrived from http://www.css-ebla.it).

Santagata, W., & Signorello, E. G. (2000). Contingent valuation and cultural policy design: The case of Napoli Musei Aperti. *Journal of Cultural Economics, 24*, 181–204.

Scott, A.J. (2000). *The Cultural Economy of Cities*. London: SAGE Publications.

Scott, A.J. (2005). *On Hollywood. The place, the industry*. Princeton and Oxford: Princeton University Press.

Simon, H. A. (1986). How managers express their creativity. *Across The Board, 23*, 11–16.

The Work Foundation DCMS, Department of Culture, Media and Sport. (2007). "*Staying Ahead: the economic performance of the UK creative Industries*", UK.

Throsby, D. (2000). *Economics and culture, trad. it. Economia e Cultura*. Bologna: Il Mulino.

Toffler, A. (1980). *The third wave*. New York: Bantam Books.

Torino Internazionale. (2005). *Piano Strategico*. downloadable: www.torino-internazionale.org.

Tornqvist, G. (1983). *Creativity and the renewal of regional life*. in A. Buttimer (Ed.), *Creativity and Context: A Seminar Report*, 91–112, Lund Studies in Geography. B. Human Geography, No. 50 Lund: Gleerup.

Trezzini, L. (2004). Il teatro. In C. Bodo (Ed.), *Rapporto sull'economia della cultura in Italia 1990–2000*. Bologna: Il Mulino.

UNCTAD (2008). *Creative economy*, Report 2008, United Nations.

UNDP. (2005). *Human development report*. New York: UNDP.

Urfalino, P. (2004). *L'Invention de la politique culturelle*. Paris: Hachette – Pluriel.

Valentino, P. (2003). *Le trame del territorio*. Milano: Civita, Sperling Kupfner Editori.

Varine, H. (2002). *Les racines du futur*. Chalon sur Saone: Asdic.

Wenger, E. (1998). *Communities of Practice: Learning, Meaning, and Identity*. Cambridge: Cambridge University Press.

The manufacturer's authorised representative in the EU is Springer Nature Customer Service Centre GmbH, Europaplatz 3, 69115 Heidelberg, Germany. If you have any concerns regarding our products, please contact ProductSafety@springernature.com

Printed and bound by CPI Group (UK) Ltd, Croydon, CR0 4YY
30/09/2026
02225608-0008